How to make
Bookshelves
& Cabinets

By the Editors of Sunset Books
and Sunset Magazine

Lane Publishing Co.,
Menlo Park, California

Edited by Donald W. Vandervort

Design and Illustrations: Ted Martine

Front cover: Pegged-together shelving
system is described on pages 62 and 63.
Photography by Norman A. Plate.
Design by Roger Flanagan

Back cover: Photographs by Ells Marugg

Executive Editor, Sunset Books: David E. Clark

Second Printing January 1975

Contents

An excellent companion to this volume is *Sunset Ideas for Storage*, which features hundreds of ways to solve everyday storage problems.

Before you start
Think of organization, storage, display

Most of us are collectors. We collect everything from A to Z—from art objects to zoom lenses. As collectibles accumulate, we find we need places to organize, store, or display them. Although some people choose to buy the necessary units, many like to save money and exercise a bit of creativity by making their own. This fact is shown by the great popularity of do-it-yourself shelving hardware. What seems to be lacking, though, is a source of ideas for easy-to-make contemporary shelving and storage that offers do-it-yourselfers a chance to express their individuality. Isn't this why you're reading *How to Make Bookshelves and Cabinets?*

Even if you've never handled a saw, you can learn to make storage and display units. The following pages tell the inexperienced carpenter everything he needs to know about buying materials, using tools, and constructing bookshelves and cabinets.

FIGURING YOUR NEEDS

Scan the various rooms of your home. How many areas could gain from additional storage or display? Could books, plants, and art objects be better displayed in the living room? Could music components and records be more conveniently organized? Could household paraphernalia be stored more efficiently? Storage and display furniture can fill these needs.

Appearance isn't everything. Don't choose a design for its good looks alone. First test its merit with the following questions:

Will it cover all the bases? Be sure the design will meet your needs. Consider the sizes, shapes, and weights of the things you'll put in or on the unit. If it is shelving, consider whether or not it should be adjustable.

Should it be permanent or movable? By nailing or screwing part of the unit to a wall or ceiling, you can eliminate the need for cabinet backs or other supports, reducing expenses. A unit built into the wall will save space, too. On the other hand, knock-down units offer more versatility because you can reposition them or take them with you when you move. Decide which structure is most suited to your needs.

Will it be easy enough to build? Although all the projects in this book were designed with simplicity in mind, some are harder to make than others. Preview the project's construction processes to see the kind of work and tools required. Look at the more involved projects realistically, taking your time, tools, and temperament into consideration.

Does it fit within your budget? Some designs require more materials than others, and some materials are relatively expensive. Review your choices

FROM CHAOS...

carefully. High-grade materials are necessary when you plan to use a natural finish or stain; units you plan to paint can generally use lower-grade materials. For garage shelving and projects where appearance is unimportant, concentrate on building for function, using the lowest acceptable grade of material.

Will it give you any bonuses? A project may have secondary uses. Freestanding shelving units might serve as room dividers; a well-designed children's cabinet could grow with the children; a kitchen cabinet, having outlived its usefulness, might be reincarnated as garage cabinetry.

HOW TO USE THIS BOOK

Information in this book is given in the order of a woodworker's thoughts as he builds a project. If you're new to woodworking, browse through the sections that discuss materials and tool use to familiarize yourself with some fundamentals. But don't feel you have to read the book from cover to cover in order to make something. When you decide on a project, just follow its directions; it will guide you to further information if and when it is needed.

The first section discusses basic materials. It will tell you the kinds of materials available, how to choose the proper ones for your project, and how to save money when buying them. It also offers pointers for working with some of the more specialized materials.

The next section tells you how to do basic woodworking using common tools: how to lay out, cut, and fasten together wooden parts. It can help you choose the right tools for your work and can be used for every project as a guide to proper technique.

The third section applies the techniques to the specifics of making bookshelves and cabinets. Each step is carefully explained. If you want to know how to construct a basic bookshelf or cabinet, hang a door, make drawers, or fasten a unit to the wall, this is where to look. This section can be especially helpful if you're making a project that you have designed because it offers basic bookshelf and cabinetmaking techniques and suggests practical alternatives.

Last come the projects; choose one that suits your needs. Step-by-step plans tell you what to do and when to do it; tool and material lists let you know what you'll need; photographs, illustrations, and plans detail specifications and points that may be hard to visualize. A photograph or illustration shows the finished appearance. Throughout the text you may find cross-references to other parts of the book that enlarge upon materials, techniques, or procedures. Some project directions may suggest alternative woodworking methods that may better suit your skills and tools.

... TO ORDER

Selecting materials
How to get more for your money

With today's skyrocketing lumber prices, you can't afford to make mistakes. Before you buy, brief yourself on what's available and how to get it at the lowest cost. You'll find this a sure bet for curtailing unnecessary expenses.

This chapter will tell you about such general-use materials as lumber and plywood. Information on hardware, fasteners, and other materials often needed for woodworking projects is included elsewhere in the book. The table at right shows you where to look.

Where should you buy materials? Home improvement centers and lumberyards carry lumber and most kinds of hardware. A builder's supply store often has a larger stock of specialized hardware. For such partially-made wooden projects as the chopping block on page 90, try cabinetmakers. Hardwoods are most easily purchased from dealers specializing in hardwoods. You'll find dealers of plastics and other specialty items listed in the yellow pages of your phone book. Shop around. If the materials in one store don't seem to suit your needs or seem too expensive, try somewhere else.

Don't feel you have to work only with standard materials. A bit of imagination, when properly applied, can turn an unlikely material into a unique, practical piece of furniture. Keep looking for ideas, especially when you're in a hardware store. What possibilities do those buckets spark? How about the clay drainpipes? Hollow-core doors are excellent for quickie projects. Plastic sprinkler pipe, boxes and crates, canvas, lawn-furniture webbing, cardboard, rope, and chain are just a few of the out-of-the-ordinary materials used to build projects in this book. Who knows — you may even have a chance to recycle discards stuffed away in storage: that trunk given to you by your great aunt, a stack of bricks, or the carcass of an old cabinet.

SELECTING LUMBER

Although the multitude of names and types of lumber might seem overwhelming, learning the basic facts about lumber isn't really difficult. This section explains the differences between species, how to judge quality, and how lumber is graded, sized, and sold.

Species

Although hundreds of species of trees exist, relatively few produce commonly available woods. All woods are separated into two broad categories: hardwood and softwood. Although both types are used in cabinetmaking, choosing between them takes careful consideration. The difference between the two is not that one is harder. The terms specify the kind of tree the wood comes from — hardwoods from broadleafed (deciduous) trees, softwoods from evergreens (conifers). Hardwoods *are* often harder than softwoods, but not always. One clear example is balsa: although the softest of woods, it is classified as a hardwood.

Woods commonly found stacked in lumberyards are softwoods. They are often a better choice than hardwoods because they are easier to work with and considerably less expensive. If you're a beginner, consider sticking to softwoods until you gain proficiency.

Although most hardwoods are more expensive than softwoods and many must be specially ordered, they offer some advantages. Some have very handsome coloring and grain, and the hard varieties lend themselves to fine craftsmanship. Although tougher to work with than softwoods, hardwoods can be tooled to more precise joinery and given smoother finishes. And, most hardwoods hold fasteners better than softwoods and have more resistance to wear.

Beyond the hardwood-softwood distinction, all wood species differ in color, grain, strength, workability, tendency to shrink and swell, and resistance to rot and insects. The chart at right shows some common species and their basic traits (all may not be available in your area). Redwood and cedar "heartwood" are the best for outdoor use because they naturally resist rot and insects.

Quality

The quality (strength and appearance) of lumber greatly affects cost. In fact, high-quality lumber can cost three or four times more than low-quality lumber. Although you wouldn't want to select lumber that isn't good enough for the job, you can minimize unnecessary expenses by determining the lowest *acceptable* grade. Here's what someone with an eye for quality looks for:

Grain. A board's grain configuration and direction depend upon the fathering tree's species and growth, and the methods used to mill it into boards. All trees produce "straight grain" and "cross grain" woods. Straight grain, the strongest, has wood fibers running parallel to a board's sides. Cross grain, whose fibers don't run parallel, weakens a board but is acceptable in small quantities. Most boards don't suffer from serious cross-grain problems but you should watch for excessive amounts.

Different methods of sawing lumber from logs create two main grain types: "vertical grain" and "flat grain." Vertical grain has a very lined appearance, whereas flat grain displays broader swirls. Flat grain lumber is more likely to react to moisture by warping or shrinking.

Defects. The size and extent of a board's defects affect the cost more than any other factor. Because defects can both weaken a board and detract from its natural appearance, they are the basis for grading standards. Below is a discussion of common defects; browse through it and determine what your project can or cannot live with.

Knots are the most common defect. A knot is either "tight" or "loose." Tight knots are sturdy; loose knots are apt to fall out, if they haven't already. (Loose knots, though, can be glued in place.) Although knots are just as strong as the rest of the wood and often tougher to cut through, the wood surrounding the knot is weak because it is cross grain. Tight knots present

CHARACTERISTICS OF WOOD

	Workability	Strength	Shrinkage	Amt. of grain pattern	Heartwood color	Relative cost
SOFTWOODS						
Cedar	B	C	A	B	D	2
Cypress	A	B	B	A	M	2
Fir	A	B	B	A	M	1
Pine	A	C	B	B	L	1
Redwood	A	B	A	A	D	1
Spruce	A	C	A	A	L	2
HARDWOODS						
Ash	B	A	B	B	L	7
Birch	A	A	C	B	L	7
Beech	B	A	C	B	M	3
Cherry	B	A	B	A	D	5
Mahogany	B	A	A	B	D	4
Maple	B	A	C	B	L	7
Oak	B	A	C	B	L	7
Poplar	B	B	B	A	M	3
Walnut	B	A	B	A	D	10
Teak	B	A	A	A	D	10

A: Excellent **B:** Good **C:** Acceptable
L: Light **M:** Medium **D:** Dark
Cost scaled from **1** to **10** (least to most)

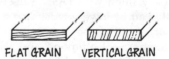

FLAT GRAIN   VERTICAL GRAIN

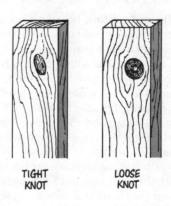

TIGHT KNOT   LOOSE KNOT

no problem where you plan to paint; just fill in irregularities and sand lightly first (page 54). For some projects, knots can be attractive when left in view.

Checks, splits, and shakes (see sketch) are the three main types of separations in wood. Checks are shallow crevasses across growth rings. Splits, the big brother of checks, extend all the way through the wood. Shakes are separations between growth rings. The size and location of these defects determine the lumber's suitability for your needs. In some cases, you can cut them off the board or fill them with patching compound.

CHECK   SPLIT   SHAKE

Pitch pockets, commonly found in pine, spruce, and Douglas fir, are openings that ooze pitch, a resin found in certain evergreens. Filling pitch pockets is difficult because the pitch usually bleeds through. If you decide to use a board with pitch pockets, clean away the pitch with turpentine. Then shellac the surface before finishing.

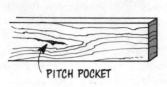

PITCH POCKET

Bowing, crooking, twisting, and cupping are defects in the shape of the board caused by exposure to moisture or improper drying methods. When selecting lumber, sight down the ends of the boards for these problems; they are not included in grading standards. If a board twists or bows, select another.

BOW   TWIST

Moisture content. Freshly cut ("green") lumber must be dried before use so that it won't expand and contract as it dries naturally. For the projects in this book, only use "kiln dried" lumber. Otherwise, the lumber may acquire some of the moisture-caused defects mentioned above — *after* you get it home.

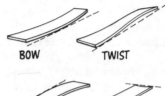

CROOK   CUP

Grading

Grading standards differ for hardwoods and softwoods. In general, the standards determine how large the defects may be and how many will be acceptable. Be sure to decide upon the appearance you wish the project to have before selecting a particular grade. High-grade lumber is right for projects that will have a transparent finish but can be extravagant for projects that will be painted.

Hardwood grading is complex. Determined by the National Lumber Association, the grading process focuses on the number of cuts necessary to produce a given size of lumber. The permissible defects vary with each grade. "Firsts" and "Seconds," the top two grades, usually combine into one grade called "FAS" (Firsts and Seconds). Unless specified otherwise, orders are usually filled with FAS. "Selects" is the third grade of hardwood lumber, followed by lower grades that are generally undesirable. These, from fair to poor, are "Number 1 Common," "Number 2 Common," "Sound Wormy," "Number 3A Common," and "Number 3B Common." Both sides of a board are graded; a board having only one side meeting FAS standards is "FAS 1 face." Choose this grade if only one side will be visible.

Knots and defects *characterize low grades (lower board). Wood free of defects (top board) can cost double.*

Softwood grading, based on U.S. Department of Commerce standards, varies with lumber manufacturing associations. "B and Better" or "1 and 2 Clear" demands wood that is free of knots and blemishes. This grade is excellent for a project that will be given a transparent finish. "C Select" may have slight knots or defects—it too is fine for a transparent finish. "D Select" may have a small knot or defect; the defect can be cut out or the piece can be given an opaque finish. "Number 1 Common" allows a few tight knots. These can be sealed and the piece painted. "Number 2 Common" has more knots and blemishes. Again, these are easily remedied ("Number 2 Pine" is often used for bookshelf boards). "Number 3 Common" has loose knots and holes but is satisfactory for nonvisible shelving. "Number 4 Common" and "Number 5 Common" are very low grades. A good, money-saving trick when you need short, high-quality boards is to cut clear pieces from lower grades.

Regarding grading terminology: *the softwood grading terms discussed at left are not used by all lumberyards for all species. Some go by variations like "Select Heart," "Construction," "Standard and Better," and "Utility." Other differences exist. Rather than attempt to learn all these names, judge the quality of lumber by its appearance if in doubt about any of the terminology.*

Lumber sizing

Hardwood lumber is normally available in odd lengths and sizes. It is sold by the lineal foot, board foot, and sometimes by the pound. If you need hardwood for a particular job, it will cost less if you simply specify the footage you need. The lumberman will sell you what he has in stock that will fill your requirement with the least waste.

Softwood lumber is sold by the board foot or lineal foot. Dimensions of common boards are specified in inches; this is called a board's "nominal size." The inch designation is given to lumber before it is dried and planed smooth. True size depends upon whether the pieces are rough or planed smooth, green or dry. Rough lumber is usually very close to the nominal size; finished lumber is always considerably less (see chart). Rough lumber is generally unacceptable for use in building bookshelves and cabinets — it is splintery and often too moist. To get a rough effect you can have lumber resawn, giving it one smooth side and one saw-textured side, but the cost of having it specially cut is usually high. Many lumberyards keep a small stock of reasonably-priced resawn lumber on hand (it's used for exterior board-and-batten siding).

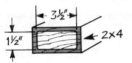

A "2x4" IS NOT EXACTLY 2 INCHES BY 4 INCHES. LIKE ALL MILLED LUMBER, IT SHRINKS AND IS PLANED TO A SMALLER SIZE. (SEE THE CHART AT RIGHT.)

STANDARD DIMENSIONS OF FINISHED LUMBER

SIZE TO ORDER	SURFACED (Actual Size)
1 x 2	¾ " x 1½ "
1 x 3	¾ " x 2½ "
1 x 4	¾ " x 3½ "
1 x 6	¾ " x 5½ "
1 x 8	¾ " x 7¼ "
1 x 10	¾ " x 9¼ "
1 x 12	¾ " x 11¼ "
2 x 2	1½ " x 1½ "
2 x 3	1½ " x 2½ "
2 x 4	1½ " x 3½ "
2 x 6	1½ " x 5½ "
2 x 8	1½ " x 7¼ "
2 x 10	1½ " x 9¼ "
2 x 12	1½ " x 11¼ "

Thickness of 3" and 4" lumber is same as respective widths above.

TABLE FOR CONVERTING LINEAL TO BOARD FEET

NOMINAL SIZE	LINEAL FEET								
	8	10	12	14	16	18	20	22	24
1 x 4	2⅔	3⅓	4	4⅔	5⅓	6	6⅔	7⅓	8
1 x 6	4	5	6	7	8	9	10	11	12
1 x 8	5⅓	6⅔	8	9⅓	10⅔	12	13⅓	14⅔	16
1 x 10	6⅔	8⅓	10	11⅔	13⅓	15	16⅔	18⅓	20
1 x 12	8	10	12	14	16	18	20	22	24
2 x 4	5⅓	6⅔	8	9⅓	10⅔	12	13⅓	14⅔	16
2 x 6	8	10	12	14	16	18	20	22	24
2 x 8	10⅔	13⅓	16	18⅔	21⅓	24	26⅔	29⅓	32
2 x 10	13⅓	16⅔	20	23⅓	26⅔	30	33⅓	36⅔	40
2 x 12	16	20	24	28	32	36	40	44	48
4 x 4	10⅔	13⅓	16	18⅔	21⅓	24	26⅔	29⅓	32

Formula for computing board feet: thickness in inches x width in feet x length in feet = number of board feet.

1x2, 1x3, 2x2, and 2x3 are sold by lineal foot.

SELECTING PLYWOOD

Plywood is an excellent building material. A manufactured material, it has several advantages over lumber: availability in very large sheets, exceptional strength, and high resistance to warp. An odd number of thin wood layers called "veneers" are glued together to form plywood sheets. Each veneer's grain runs perpendicular to the adjacent veneer's.

Exterior and interior types are available. Exterior plywood is bonded with glues that won't delaminate even when boiled in water, but it is usually slightly more expensive than interior plywood. Unless the project will be exposed to excessive moisture or humidity, it's thrifty to choose interior plywood.

All plywood is divided into one of two categories: softwood or hardwood. The difference is in the species of wood covering the outer faces of a panel. Although both types are used in cabinetmaking, hardwood plywood is usually considerably more expensive than softwood.

Softwood plywood

The most commonly used plywood is softwood, usually Douglas fir. Other softwood species include Western hemlock, redwood, cedar, Sitka spruce, Southern yellow pine, Western larch pine, and white fir. All plywood comes in standard 4' by 8' sheets. Larger sizes are available, and some stores sell quarter or half sheets. Standard thicknesses of softwood plywood are ¼", ⅜", ½", ⅝", and ¾" (5/16", ⅞", and 1⅛" are more difficult to find).

Plywood is graded according to the appearance of the front and back faces. From finest to poorest, softwood grades are designated "N," "A," "B," "C," and "D." "N" is defect free with uniform color. Use it only where you want a flawless natural finish. "A" grade has neatly-made repairs and is excellent for use where you want a natural finish. "B" surfaces may have oval-shaped repair plugs and tight knots. A good panel from this grade can be finished naturally; poorer panels should be painted. "C" plys can have knots slightly larger than 1" and small splits. One grade, known as "C-plugged," is more improved and good for painting. "D" grade, the poorest, has larger knots and splits; use this grade where it will be hidden from view. Both faces of a panel are graded — "A-A" would be excellent where seen from both sides; "A-D" is fine where only one side will show. Panels stamped "shop" have been mismanufactured — if you don't need a full panel, perhaps you can salvage enough usable material from a shop-grade panel (beware — some defects are not visible). Buying shop-grade or damaged panels can save you dollars.

Hardwood plywood

The main types of domestic hardwoods veneered on plywood sheets are ash, birch, black walnut, cherry, gum, maple, and oak. Several imported woods, such as lauan, mahogany, teak, and rosewood, are also available in some areas. Like softwood plywood, the common sheet size is 4' by 8'. Thicknesses are ⅛", 3/16", ¼", ⅜", ½", ⅝", ¾", and 1". Because hardwoods are relatively scarce, lumberyards do not carry all species and thicknesses of hardwood plywood.

In the hardwood plywood category, there are two variations on the plywood theme. One type of hardwood plywood has a core of extra-thick veneer or solid wood. The solid-wood type is called "lumber-core plywood." Another type has a particle-board core (see more about particle board on page 12). Lumber-core plywood is often used for such projects as table tops or doors that specify butt hinges (the edges can be worked like solid lumber). Particle-board core is very strong with greater dimensional

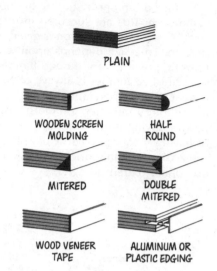

PLAIN

WOODEN SCREEN MOLDING

HALF ROUND

MITERED

DOUBLE MITERED

WOOD VENEER TAPE

ALUMINUM OR PLASTIC EDGING

Plywood edges are sometimes unappealing. When you don't want the natural, laminated look of veneered edges, mask them with veneer tape or moldings. Plain edges can also be painted.

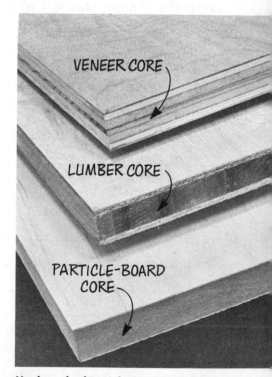

VENEER CORE

LUMBER CORE

PARTICLE-BOARD CORE

Hardwood plywood cores can differ. The three main types are veneer, lumber, and particle board.

stability. It is also less expensive but quite heavy.

As with softwood plys, both faces of a hardwood plywood panel are graded. Grades of veneers are Specialty Grade ("SP"), made to order; Premium Grade ("#1"), well-matched veneers, uniform color; Good Grade ("#1," too), uniform color and grain; Sound Grade ("#2"), veneers not matched for color or grain and pinhole knots but no open defects; Utility Grade ("#3"), several kinds of defects permitted but fine for painting; and Backing Grade ("#4"), generally used only in concealed areas.

Other veneered materials

Several special-purpose veneered materials are available. Here are the types useful for cabinetmaking:

Grooved (Texture 1-11) plywood. Specially-cut ⅜-inch-wide grooves run the length of these plywood panels, spaced apart from each other at 2", 4", or 8" centers. Presently, grooved plywood is available only in one size: ⅝". Though an exterior plywood, it can be used for making bookshelves (see page 68).

Resin-overlaid plywood. This type consists of resin-impregnated sheeting, permanently fused to standard exterior plywood. Because grain raise and checking do not show, it offers an excellent surface on which to paint. Medium-density panels are most commonly used for painting. High-density panels are attractive even when left unfinished.

Wall paneling. Several types of prefinished plywood and hardboard wall paneling are available. Though not very structural, they are an inexpensive solution where large sheets of decorative material are necessary.

Hardwood veneer. Many different species of hardwoods are available in rolls of very thin veneer. Standard widths of the rolled sheets range from 8" to 24"; lengths run from 1' to 8'. The relatively expensive veneers are usually applied to plywood surfaces using contact cement, a job that requires some practice.

Hardboard *sports several thicknesses, textures, and colors. The two panels at top are perforated. The lower panels show smooth and textured faces.*

SELECTING HARDBOARD

Hardboard consists of tiny wood fibers bonded under heat and pressure into dense wooden sheets. For added moisture resistance and strength (but less flexibility), some hardboard is "tempered" with thermal-setting materials baked into place. As with plywood sheets, standard sizes are 4' by 8' to 16'. Surfaces are 1/12, 1/10, ⅛, 5/32, 3/16, 7/32, ¼, 5/16, and 7/16 thick. The two most commonly sold are ⅛" and ¼". Hardboard comes in dark brown, gray, and blond; it can be smooth, textured, or perforated (perforated hardboard is used for hang-up storage walls — a wide variety of specially-sized hooks and supports fit into its perforations).

Hardboard's density makes it one of the most dent-resistant of all sheet products; it's excellent for covering flat areas that must take wear. The smooth finish (it has no knots or defects) is ideal for painting and will not check or split in weather. Because it has no grain, hardboard has strength in all directions. Ordinary shop tools are used to work hardboard (though cutting tools are dulled rapidly).

Problems include its inability to hold nails or screws securely (although you can nail or screw through it into wood), the fact that it expands and contracts with changes in moisture (presenting problems with joints), and a sometimes cold, hard appearance. Its most common uses in cabinetmaking are for sliding cabinet doors, drawer bottoms, and cabinet backs. The photo at right shows perforated hardboard in use.

Perforated hardboard, *combined with plug-in hangers, makes an excellent hang-up storage board.*

PARTICLE BOARD ("CHIPBOARD")

Made from particles of wood impregnated with glue and pressed into sheets, particle board has a speckled appearance in contrast to the smooth look of hardboard. Even so, particle board has a smoother surface than standard Douglas fir plywood. Sheet size is 4' by 8'; thicknesses run from ¼" to ¾". It is available in both interior and exterior varieties. Standard tools are used to work particle board, but cutting tools are dulled quickly.

Particle board is an excellent material to use under certain circumstances because it is one of the least expensive building materials. What are the right conditions for using it? Particle board is suitable when applying an opaque finish, when its heavy weight is unimportant, and when you will not need to screw or nail into it (because of its brittle composition, particle board isn't good at holding screws and nails; however, you can nail or screw through it into wood). Glue and bolts work best with particle board. Particle board makes first-rate low-cost painted shelving. You can smooth its pitted edges by using a paste filler and sanding. Don't finish particle board with water-base paint; the water tends to soak into the wood, causing the grain to raise.

Particle board *sells mostly in these sizes: ¼", ½", and ¾". The bottom ¾" panel has plastic laminate surface.*

WOODEN MOLDINGS

Moldings can turn a plain wooden surface into a work of art. They can hide inaccuracies in joints, and some of the larger sizes can form main structural elements of a project. Scores of different shapes and styles are available from basic screen moldings to ornate picture-frame moldings. A few of the more useful profiles are shown at right, along with their common names.

Those who work with moldings know that precise cutting is richly rewarded. A fine-toothed backsaw in a miter box (see page 18) is ideal for cutting 45° miters, and a coping saw (page 19) cuts matching curvatures well. Moldings are fastened in place with glue and finishing nails or brads (set nailheads below the surface).

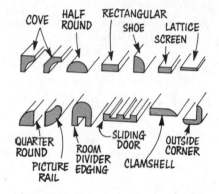

Wooden moldings *have many shapes.*

DOWELING AND ROUNDS

Several of the projects in this book incorporate dowels and pegs as major design elements. The projects on pages 62 and 70 are two good examples. Doweling is basically used for strengthening joints (page 27), but the smooth, even appearance of a round length of wood can also make home-crafted projects look more professional.

Usually made from maple or oak, doweling comes in diameters from ⅛" to 1" (graduated by 1/16"), and 3' or 4' lengths. "Rounds" or "baluster" (pine or fir dowels) come in diameters up to 1¾", and lengths up to 20'. Typical doweling and rounds are shown at right.

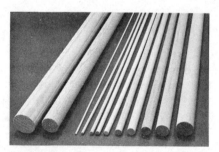

Doweling *runs from ⅛" to 1". Softwood rounds, two at left, are 1¾", 1".*

ALUMINUM MOLDINGS

Aluminum can add a touch of metallic sheen to projects, at the same time contributing qualities of light weight and strength. Several shapes of do-it-yourself aluminum are available; they can be worked with fine-toothed saws and standard drills. Some of the common molding shapes are shown at right; aluminum sheets are also available.

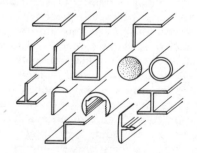

Aluminum moldings *are easy to use.*

EASY-TO-USE PLASTICS

Two plastics are often used in cabinetmaking: plastic laminate and acrylic plastic. Laminate is used most often, covering hundreds of thousands of kitchen cabinet and bathroom vanity counters. Acrylic plastic, however, is popular for sliding cabinet doors and extrusions; and it can be used like moldings.

Plastic laminate

A prefinished surface that is resistant to impact, scratches, grease and stains, moisture, and low heats, plastic laminate deserves its popularity. Yet many homeowners have shied away from laying plastic laminate themselves, thinking the job beyond the skills of do-it-yourselfers. On the contrary, when you follow directions, plastic laminate isn't difficult to lay, offers a professional-looking surface, and hides inaccuracies in construction. At least a hundred different textures and colors exist. Counters and plywood sheets prefinished with plastic laminate are also available.

Acrylic sheets and extrusions

Buy acrylic plastic at paint and wallpaper stores, hobby shops, lumber dealers, hardware stores, or plastic dealers. The sheets and moldings can be either translucent or transparent and just about every color and tint under the rainbow. Typical molding shapes are flat, round, and square tubing, and round and square bar. Acrylic plastic is relatively expensive, but the sheets make reasonably-priced, unbreakable sliding cabinet doors. Prices vary according to the colors and sizes. Clear plastic is the least expensive but the most likely to show scratches under heavy use.

   Anyone can work with acrylics. A scribing tool is made for quickly cutting ⅛" and ¼" sheets — you just score several times along the cutting line, run a ¾" dowel beneath the line, hold the sheet down with one hand, and press on the piece you're cutting off with the other (hold hands about 2" from intended break). This method doesn't work for cutting off strips narrower than 1½".

   A circular saw equipped with a plywood cutting blade (carbide is best) also cuts acrylics. Set the teeth so they protrude only slightly through the material and slowly feed the plastic into the blade. Leave the paper backing on for this and wear goggles. Saber saws, bandsaws, and coping saws with fine-toothed blades will cut curves. Slow-speed drills will bore holes (back the holes with a scrap to prevent chipping). Edges can be filed, sanded, or given a high luster with wet-and-dry sandpaper and a buffing compound.

To cut acrylic plastic, *first score the sheets several times along a straight-edge, using a knife made for the purpose.*

Then break *the sheet over a ¾" dowel, pushing down with your hands about 2" from each side of the intended break.*

LAYING COUNTERTOP PLASTIC

With patience and care, plastic laminate can be reasonably easy to install. The material should be cut to exact size and then bonded to a plywood base (usually ¾") with contact cement (page 28).

   To cut the plastic, first scribe along the cut-off line with a sharp tool (mark the panel to cut good side up with a handsaw or table saw, good side down with a portable circular saw or radial-arm saw). Cut along the line with a handsaw (12 to 15 teeth per inch) at a low angle or use a power saw with a plywood cutting blade (a tungsten-carbide blade is recommended). If you plan to put plastic strips around the sides of the project top, allow ⅛" overlap on all edges (it is best to cement sides in place before marking the top for correct fit).

   The cemented surfaces will create an inseparable bond once they touch, so practice the laying processes without glue. Be sure the fit will be exact. Then spread contact cement on the two bonding surfaces. Let the cement dry thoroughly. Completely cover the cemented plywood with a large piece of wrapping paper and lay the plastic on the paper (glued side down). The dry glue shouldn't stick to the paper. Align all the edges properly; then gradually pull the paper out, pressing the plastic into place as you go. If it starts going down improperly, stop. Try to get your fingers under the piece to pry it up. Remove any accumulations of adhesive on the surfaces with benzine or naphtha and try again.

   Once it's laid, you can trim the plastic's edges flush with a router (see page 25) and special trimming bit, trim it with a special hand-operated trimming tool that works like a plane, or simply file the edges smooth with a fine-toothed file and cover them with aluminum edging.

Using tools
How to lay out, cut, & assemble materials

Don't let an empty tool box discourage you from woodworking. The bare necessities — a rule, hammer, saw, and drill — will be enough for many of the projects in this book. You can get these tools for less than $20 in a hardware store or for practically nothing at a flea market or garage sale. (If you buy secondhand tools, pass over those that look cheaply made. Poor tools are a poor investment.)

For some projects, sophisticated tools are necessary. Generally speaking, the better the tools, the easier the work. If you lack a particular tool but would rather not spend the money to buy it, perhaps you can borrow or lease it from a local tool rental. If you need a costly tool for only a limited time, it's worthwhile to rent it.

Constructing most projects requires three main procedures: laying out the dimensions, cutting the pieces to size and shape, and assembling the parts. These procedures are not necessarily separate — don't cut all the parts before beginning to assemble them. Instead, measure and cut pieces as the assembling progresses so you can adjust for misfittings.

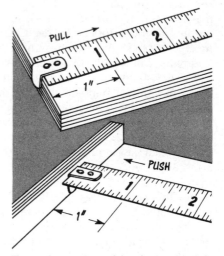

Laying out a project

When building a project of your own design, you'll need to draw up a detailed set of plans and figure a list of materials (be sure to account for stock types and sizes of available materials). For this book's projects, though, these steps have been taken for you; your first working steps will be measuring and marking materials where you will cut, fasten, drill, or shape them. Some basic measuring, marking, and gauging methods and tools are discussed below.

Tape measure's end hook should slide back and forth slightly for precise inside and outside measurements.

HOW TO USE MEASURING TOOLS

Most important in getting a project off on the right foot is careful measuring. Tight-fitting joinery for fine cabinets demands measuring and cutting to within 1/32" or 1/64" of proper measurements. Less critical bookshelf boards and pieces can be cut to within 1/16". For rough measuring, you can use a wooden yardstick or ruler; for more precise work, use a metal tape measure, a metal yardstick, or a square's blade. Whenever possible during construction, use one material to transfer measurements to another. No matter what tools you use, measure twice and cut only once.

Tape measure. You can buy a compact, flexible steel tape for less than $5. How do you choose one? Pick a tape container that measures exactly 2" or 3" along its base to make measuring between two surfaces easy. The tape's end hook should be loosely riveted so that it will slide the distance

Transfer measurements from one material to another when possible.

of its own thickness, adjusting that thickness for precise "inside" and "outside" measurements. If you buy a tape that automatically recoils into its case, check to see if it can be locked in an extended position. (When using a recoiling tape, push the last few inches into the case, saving the end hook from slamming against the case.)

Squares. The blade of a combination or framing square excels for making precise, short measurements; the versatility of these multiple-use tools offers several bonuses. Shown at the bottom of the page are some of the jobs they can do. If you don't own a combination square, strongly consider buying one. It could be one of your most-used tools.

Compass or wing dividers. A simple, stiff schoolroom compass works for limited measuring jobs and draws circles or arcs as discussed under "Marking Lines." Wing dividers are more precise but cost more (they have a knurled screw that holds the legs in place). Use these tools to transfer small measurements or to step off equal marks.

Wing dividers or compass duplicates irregularities of one surface on another.

MARKING LINES ACCURATELY

Laying out most projects will require drawing lines — some straight, some curved, some at a particular angle. The first tool needed for this is a pointed scribe or a good sharp pencil. A scribe marks a more precise line, but the scratch it leaves cannot be erased as can a pencil line. Some of the following tools may be helpful for guiding your pencil or scribe in drawing straight, curved, or angled lines.

Straight lines. Any straight tool can help you draw straight lines: a square, a level, or a yardstick. A yardstick is especially handy for long lines, but only if it is straight and has a hard edge. Sight down its length to make sure it isn't slightly warped or curved. Although many paint stores give yardsticks away, it's wise to buy the more accurate metal ones.

Curved lines. As already mentioned above, either wing dividers or a compass can draw arcs or small circles. They also duplicate irregularities of one surface (like a wall) to another surface (like a board that must fit flush), as shown at top. For drawing large-radius circles or curves, tack one end of a yardstick to the material (see photo).

Angles. The versatile combination square aids in marking several types of lines: a precise right angle (90°), a miter (45°), or a straight line. A sliding T-bevel will duplicate any angle.

Draw large circle or curve by tacking one end of yardstick to material.

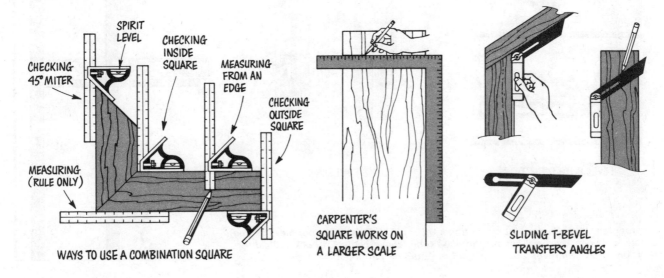

WAYS TO USE A COMBINATION SQUARE

- CHECKING 45° MITER
- SPIRIT LEVEL
- CHECKING INSIDE SQUARE
- MEASURING FROM AN EDGE
- CHECKING OUTSIDE SQUARE
- MEASURING (RULE ONLY)

CARPENTER'S SQUARE WORKS ON A LARGER SCALE

SLIDING T-BEVEL TRANSFERS ANGLES

GAUGING TRUE LEVEL OR PLUMB

Because houses are built "level" (at the same horizontal plane, for instance, as the surface of water), horizontal parts of a cabinet or bookshelf should be level and vertical supports "plumb" (straight up and down), or the unit will lean. You can find a good reference for true level and plumb by using any of the following methods (illustrated at right):

Spirit level (A). If you own or can borrow a carpenter's spirit level, you have the problem solved in a very sophisticated fashion. The level is a straight tool having two or more small, enclosed tubes along its length — one set gauges level, another finds plumb. You hold the level against the structure and adjust the structure until the bubble in the appropriate tube is framed precisely by the hairlines on the tube.

Some combination squares (**B**) have a small spirit level in their handles. If you buy a square for measuring or marking purposes, consider getting this kind. Because of the combination square's short length, the spirit level isn't accurate enough for all jobs, but it still can be useful.

Plumb bob (C). Simply a pointed weight at the end of a string, a plumb bob is suspended from above — its weight hangs straight down, offering a perfect reference for plumb. Use one by suspending it from the ceiling or some other high surface next to the object being adjusted; let the weight's point dangle a fraction of an inch over the floor. Once the weight stops swinging back and forth, the string it hangs from is exactly plumb.

Improvise. Find true level by holding a 90° square in alignment with a plumb bob's string (**D**) or align the square with a plumb wall (**E**). Or try hanging any kind of weight from the end of a string; the string will indicate plumb. As a last resort, try measuring from each end of each shelf to the floor or ceiling (**F**). Measurements should match.

NOT LEVEL (NOT PLUMB)   LEVEL (PLUMB)

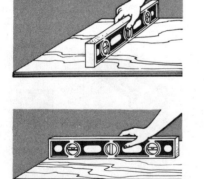

LEVEL BOTH DIRECTIONS   PLUMB BOTH SIDES

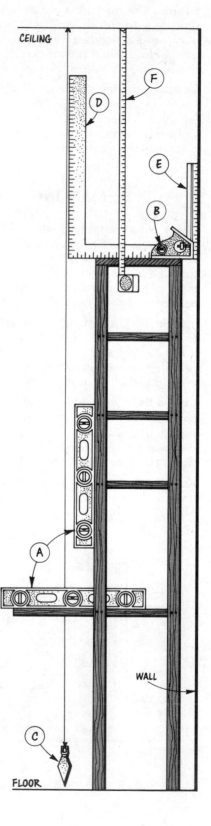

A carpenter's level *is excellent for finding level or plumb. Be sure the bubble is framed exactly between the hairlines on the glass tube (above center). Check both directions on surface for level (above left) or both sides for plumb (above right).*

Cutting wood

Your ability to properly cut can make or break a project's success. It's worth investing time and patience in cutting carefully and accurately.

Almost all lumberyards do cutting for a small fee. Finding out which lumberyards in your area offer this service and at what cost can really pay off, especially when you have a 4' by 8' sheet of plywood to cart home and cut up. If you ask the dealer to make cuts, plan your cutting diagrams so he makes the longest ones. Be sure to specify whether or not the measurements must be exact.

Sawing isn't the only way to cut into wood. Other cutting processes discussed in this section include drilling holes, chiseling, planing, and abrading. The information on sawing is divided into two main sections: cutting straight lines and cutting curves. Though these two jobs usually require different tools, all sawing jobs have certain traits in common.

The number of teeth per inch along a saw blade determines the kind of cut it makes. The fewer the teeth, the rougher the cut — many teeth make a smooth cut. For almost all cabinet work, use smooth-cutting blades — these will minimize splintering away the cut's backside. The best handsaws for cutting plywood and finish work have from 8 to 12 teeth per inch. Various types of plywood-cutting blades are made for doing this kind of work with power saws.

Where saw teeth exit, wood will tend to splinter and break away. A couple of tricks that will help prevent this from happening are shown at right. The side of the wood that tends to break away will depend upon the saw you use. Some have upward-cutting blades; others cut downward. Look to see the direction the teeth are pointed — that is, the direction they cut into and exit from wood. Cut good-side-up when using a handsaw, table saw, or radial-arm saw. If you use a portable circular saw or saber saw, cut the wood good-side down.

Don't forget to support both halves of the piece you're cutting. Otherwise, the saw will bind and, as you near the end of the cut, the unsupported piece will break away. If the saw binds anyway, stick a screwdriver in the end of the cut to spread it open.

SAWING STRAIGHT LINES

The simplest and least expensive tool for sawing straight lines is the handsaw. Two basic types are available: the ripsaw and the crosscut saw. The ripsaw is made to cut only in line with wood grain. Choose the crosscut saw instead; it is better for general cutting. Other saws designed for cutting straight lines include the backsaw, power circular saw, radial-arm saw, and table saw. The saber saw (also called a "portable jigsaw") is versatile enough to cut both straight and curved lines accurately.

Crosscut saw. The crosscut saw can do almost any straight woodcutting job. If you don't have a power saw, it will be the most important saw in your tool collection for this book's projects.

The length of crosscut blades varies from about 20" to 26". A 26" blade is a good choice. Crosscut saws do about 75 percent of their cutting on the downstroke and 25 percent on the upstroke. Start a cut by slowly drawing the saw *up* a few times to make a notch or kerf. If you make a full kerf

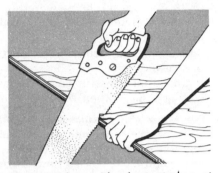

Begin sawing *with short strokes at blade's wide end, then progress to smooth, long, generous strokes.*

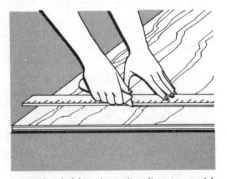

Score backside *of cutting line to avoid splintering the wood where teeth exit. Or try taping line's backside with masking tape. Better yet, back the cut with a scrap and cut both together.*

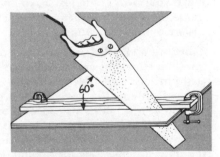

To cut straight, *guide the saw against a board clamped along the cutting line. Saw lumber at 45° angle; cut plywood and other sheet materials at 60°.*

about ½" into the far edge of the board, it will help guide the blade straight for the remainder of the cut. For clean, straight cuts with a minimum of effort, grasp the handle firmly and cut as shown on the preceding page, your forearm in line with the teeth.

Backsaw. A backsaw, for finish work, cuts straight lines precisely. If you won't be doing much critical finish cutting, you can probably get along without one. Rectangular in shape, the fine-cutting backsaw derives its name from a metal reinforcing strip that runs the spine's length to keep it from bowing.

The backsaw shown is being used in a wooden miter box to cut a piece of molding at an accurate angle. Backsaws are available in lengths from 12" to 28", but for the home workshop a 12" or 14" saw is best. Twelve teeth per inch is right unless you are doing very fine work, in which case a dovetail backsaw works best. Dovetail saws have shorter, thinner blades with finer teeth, and their handles are straight — shaped much like the handles of screwdrivers.

Unlike the crosscut saw, the blade of a backsaw is held parallel to the cutting surface when you are sawing.

Power portable circular saw. Although the portable circular saw can probably cut about five times faster than a handsaw, it is a dangerous tool that requires extreme caution. Unless you plan to do a lot of cutting in the future and have learned how to handle one of these saws, don't rush out and buy one.

As a general rule, power tools produce faster and more precise work than hand tools, after you've learned to use them properly. But a tool such as the power circular saw feels heavy, bulky, and hard to handle at first. To assist in cutting long, straight lines with one, you can make a guide like the one shown.

Remember, the blade of a circular saw cuts upward. To avoid splintering away the best side of materials, cut them best-side down. Set the blade so the teeth just protrude through the wood's surface.

A good way to cut large sheets is to lay two or three scrap 2 by 4s across two saw horses and adjust the saw foot so the blade will cut through your material and only partially through these scraps. The scraps will support the piece during the cutting, making the large piece more manageable.

Circular saws range from 6 to 10-inch-diameter sizes, and there are dozens of blade types. A 7" to 7½" saw with a combination blade (designed to do both crosscut and rip sawing) works best for most home woodworking and cabinetmaking jobs.

Saber saw (jigsaw). Although chiefly used for cutting curves, the saber saw (with a guide as described below) cuts surprisingly straight lines. A guide is usually furnished with the tool for making parallel cuts a short distance from a board's edge. For cutting across panels or wide surfaces, you can make your own guide just as you do for a circular saw. An alternative is to guide the saw's base plate against a straightedge that's clamped a measured distance from the cutting line.

Table saw and radial-arm saw. Two other large power saws that are excellent for cabinetmaking are the table saw and the radial-arm saw. These tools perform very accurately and can be a blessing for the woodworker who does a lot of cutting. The table saw is a power circular saw that is permanently mounted in a table. Instead of moving the blade through the wood, the wood is fed to the blade. Locking rip fences (bars that clamp across the table) and miter gauges (braces that run in slots in the table) make the table saw the most accurate saw for ripping or for crosscutting short pieces of wood. Blades can be changed to fit the job, or a combination blade can be used for general-purpose work.

The radial-arm saw is another circular saw that uses the same blade types

Backsaw *in inexpensive miter box makes easy and accurate 45° and 90° cuts across small-dimension lumber.*

Homemade guide *helps circular saw cut long, straight lines easily. Make one from scrap plywood and molding.*

Saber saw *cuts straight when steered against a straightedge that's been clamped to the work piece.*

Radial-arm saw *(left) excels at cross-cutting long boards. Table saw (above) will rip a board or panel easily and crosscut short pieces of lumber.*

as the portable circular saw and table saw. The wood is positioned on a table; the motor and blade, mounted on an arm above the table, are drawn across. The saw can be raised, lowered, tilted, and even swiveled for miter cuts or rip cuts. Its greatest advantage over the table saw is its ability to crosscut long pieces.

SAWING CURVES & IRREGULAR LINES

Unlike most blades designed for cutting straight lines, a blade for cutting curves or zigzagging irregular cuts must be thin and narrow in shape and used in an almost straight up-and-down position. Four main curve-cutting saws are discussed in this section: compass saw, coping saw, saber saw, and band saw. The first two are very inexpensive handsaws; the saber saw, as already mentioned, is a most versatile electric tool; the band saw is an expensive shop tool. All four use replaceable blades.

Keyhole saw, *started in drilled hole, makes cut-out in the center of a panel.*

Keyhole saw. Also known as a "compass saw," the keyhole saw is typically used in making irregular or curved cuts and in starting cuts in the center of a board or panel from a small drilled hole. Blade lengths vary from 10" to 14". The blade is pointed at the "toe" (tip) and less than an inch wide at the "head."

The handiest type to buy comes as a kit, packaged with three interchangeable blades: one cuts broad curves or straight lines rapidly; one saws tight curves, zigzags, and cutouts; and one cuts metal. The last blade, for metal cutting, is the bargain part of the package because it saves the additional expense of buying a hacksaw. (You may have to cut metal for some cabinet-making projects.)

When cutting curves with the compass saw, cut perpendicular to the surface. Be careful with the blades; they tend to bend easily. To begin a cut-out, insert the blade in a previously drilled hole. Once you've started a long, straight cut, you can insert a regular handsaw in the cut to finish the job quickly.

Coping saw. With its thin, wiry blade held taut in a small rectangular frame, the coping saw makes thin, accurate cuts and follows tight curves with

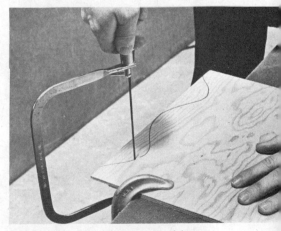

Coping saw, *limited by its metal frame, cuts lines more intricately curved than any of the other saws can cut.*

ease — but cutting is limited to surfaces that its relatively small frame will fit around.

Both wood and metal cutting blades can be inserted in a coping saw frame. For inside cuts, slip the blade through a pre-drilled hole and then reattach it to the frame. When cutting vertically in a vise, point the teeth toward the handle and cut on the pull stroke. If you're working on something supported horizontally, as on a sawhorse, point the teeth away from the handle and cut on the push stroke.

Saber saw (power jigsaw). Although the compass saw kit previously mentioned will get you through almost any of the curve cutting in this book, a saber saw makes curve cutting — and, in fact, almost any cutting job — perfectly painless.

The saber saw has a high-speed reciprocating motor that drives any of several interchangeable blades to cut wood, sheet metal, plastic, rubber, leather, and even electrical conduit. Depending upon how you use it, it will cut intricately-curved lines, circles, straight lines, bevels, and can make a cut-out in the center of a panel without needing a previously-drilled starting hole.

The blade of the saw shown below can be turned independently from the rest of the saw. In addition, this saw has a variable-speed trigger for greater control.

As discussed at the beginning of the section on sawing, cut with the material's best side down; the upward-cutting blade may fray the top surface as it cuts. For more instructions on proper use, see the owner's manual provided with the tool.

Band saw. This power saw has a continuous-band blade that rolls between two wheels — one above and one below the cutting platform. A narrow blade can make very tight circular cuts, and a wider, sturdier blade can cut wood over 6″ thick. Because the saw is fairly specialized, you probably won't need one for making bookshelves and cabinets, except for cutting intricately-curved decorative pieces.

Saber saw *tracks curved lines easily; blade of this one can be turned independently of the body.*

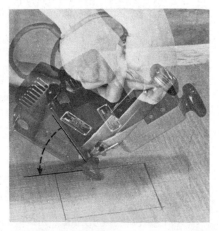

Dip *into the center of a panel to make a cut-out by tilting the saber saw forward on its toe plate, starting the motor, and slowly lowering the tool.*

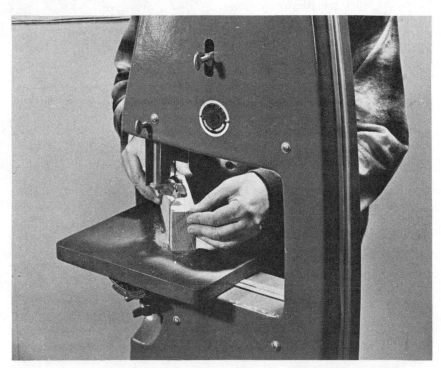

Bandsaw *is a powerful, freestanding curve cutter. You push wood into blade.*

DRILLING HOLES

A good drill is needed for many of the projects in this book. Although several kinds are discussed below, you don't need them all. In fact, you can probably get by with just one: a ¼" or ⅜" electric drill. Either of these is easy to use and, when fitted with the proper drill bit or attachment, can accomplish much more than just drilling holes.

Hand-operated drills

Three types of hand drills are commonly available: standard eggbeater type, push drill, and brace. The first two drill only small holes; the brace primarily bores large holes. Punches, awls, and twist tools, such as those shown at right, although not called "drills," are handy for quickly boring screw-starting and other small holes.

Eggbeater hand drill. If you plan on drilling only small holes and prefer not to invest a few extra dollars in an electric drill, the standard eggbeater hand drill is your best bet. It's used for drilling either metal or wood; its jaws usually take round-shank bits up to ¼" in diameter. To use the drill, simply crank the handle clockwise.

Push drill. Used for rapidly punching small holes through wooden materials, the push drill has bits that are ground with points which cut when rotated in either direction. When pushed down, a strong spring-and-spiral mechanism moves a push drill's bit clockwise; some push drills also turn the bit counterclockwise when released.

Brace. A brace and bit will drill holes from ¼" to about 2" in diameter. Made for boring only in wood, the brace is worked like a crank, the average brace having a sweep of about 10". Most braces are equipped with a ratchet (gear-like device) that allows you to bore holes even where the crank-like sweep is restricted.

Several bits and attachments other than the standard auger bit are available (see bottom photo). All of these bits and attachments lock into the brace's chuck (jaws).

To bore a hole, center the bit's point on your mark, hold the round butt knob with one hand, and turn the offset handle clockwise with the other. Don't let the butt knob rock. Apply a little pressure when starting the bit; once it has dug in, it should pull through the wood on its own.

Electric drills

An electric drill makes the job of boring much faster and easier. Because of its versatility, it qualifies as one of the most used tools in a tool box. Power drills are classified according to the maximum size bit or accessory shank they can grip. Three sizes are sold: ¼", ⅜", and ½". As the chuck size increases, the power output becomes greater. A ½" drill offers more torque power and is geared to slower speeds than a ⅜" drill; similarly, the ⅜" drill delivers more torque at a slower speed than a ¼" drill.

A standard ¼" or ⅜" drill should handle almost any of the drilling jobs you will encounter — the ⅜" is capable of fairly heavy-duty work (such as powering a hole saw) and will stand up longer under prolonged use in drilling hardwoods, metal, or concrete. If you need a ½" drill for a certain job (extensive masonry drilling, for instance), you can probably rent one.

Consider a few factors before buying a power drill. First, it's best to choose a double-insulated tool. Double insulation is designed to give you double protection from accidental electrical shock; double-insulated tools have casings of high-impact, break-resistant, nonconductive plastic. In addition, you won't need to find an adapter for a three-pronged electrical cord

Punches, awls, and twist tools efficiently bore small holes for starting screws in soft woods. Punch at far left centers holes for hinge screws. The two at right form threads for screws.

Eggbeater hand drill is easy to use.

Push drill punches holes quickly.

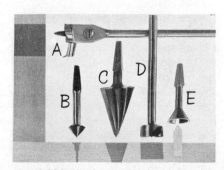

Brace and bit bores holes in wood.

Special bits for brace: **(A)** expansion bit, **(B)** countersink, **(C)** reamer, **(D)** Foerstner bit, and **(E)** dowel sharpener. After adjusting expansion bit, drill a test hole.

plug (used to ground a tool) because double-insulated tools don't have or need the extra prong.

Consider the type of trigger — what does it do? The least expensive drill has a trigger that turns the drill either on or off. A slightly more sophisticated model may have a two-speed trigger: one fast speed, one slow. The best trigger totally controls the motor's speed; the more you squeeze it, the faster the motor turns. With a variable-speed drill, you can suit the speed to the job — very handy when starting holes, drilling unusual materials, driving screws, or powering large attachments. Sophisticated triggers will also reverse the direction of the motor to pull out screws or a bit that's hopelessly stuck.

If you want to purchase a drill press (shown on the next page) or any other "fitted" accessory, be sure one is available to fit your drill.

A drill that will last and serve you well should have a 90-day warranty, an Underwriter's Laboratory certification, a durable body, 1/5 horsepower, and protection against motor burnout.

How to drill properly

The three drilling problems that crop up most often are: 1) centering the moving drill bit on its mark, 2) drilling a hole straight, and 3) keeping the wood's backside from breaking away as the drill bit pierces. Following are time-tested techniques that can help rid your work of these problems.

Keep a pointed tool handy for center punching starting holes. A couple of taps with a hammer on a large nail, nailset, or punch will leave a hole that will prevent the bit from wandering.

Unless you have a drill press or a press accessory for your power drill (facing page), drilling straight holes may be difficult. Three methods you can try are shown at right.

To keep a drill from breaking out the wood's backside, do one of two things: 1) lay or clamp a wood scrap firmly against your work piece's backside and drill through the work piece into the scrap, or 2) just before the drill pierces, flop the work piece over and finish drilling from the other side.

How do you know when the drill will penetrate? You can either buy a depth gauge made for the purpose or improvise as illustrated below.

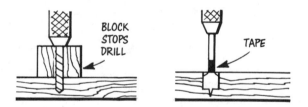

Here are a few general tips. Clamp materials down, particularly when using a power drill — the torque of a drill (especially when combined with a large spade bit, expansion bit, or hole saw) can easily wrench the wood out of your grasp. Hold the drill firmly, leaving the motor on as you remove the bit from the wood. To avoid breaking small bits, don't tilt the drill once it has entered the wood. When possible, adapt the drill speed to the job. As you drill, use generally light pressure, letting the bit do the work; excessive pressure and speed overheat the drill, make it hard to control, and ruin bits. As a general rule, avoid using bits wider than the diameter of the chuck unless drilling softwood.

Wear plastic safety goggles, especially if you're drilling brittle surfaces. Most manufacturers provide a valuable set of safety rules from the Power Tool Institute, along with useful guidelines for equipment maintenance; be sure to read these.

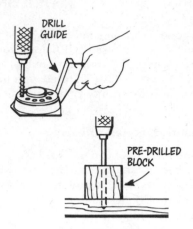

Drill straight with a commercial guide (left) or with one made from a scrap block of wood (right).

Combination square helps line up the drill when holes must be straight.

Cradle a dowel in a trough, made by cutting a V-groove into a block, to keep it from revolving while you drill.

Power drill bits and accessories

Bits and accessories make a power drill one of the most versatile, useful tools in a tool box. Only a sampling of available accessories is shown — tools that are used specifically for cabinetmaking jobs. Other drill attachments vary from hedge trimmers to water pumps.

Fractional twist bits are shown in the set at top. Their sizes are graduated in fractions of an inch. This set contains seven bits, varying by 32nds of an inch — 1/16", 3/32", 1/8", 5/32", 3/16", 7/32", and 1/4". A larger set comes in 64ths. Choose high-speed bits for a power drill; they can be used in both wood and metal. Low-speed bits will burn and dull easily. Twist bits can also be used in eggbeater hand drills.

Inexpensive spade bits, chucked into a power drill, bore 3/8" to 1 1/2" holes. For drilling both wood and plastic, they cut clean holes and seldom bind. Only use them with power drills.

Oversized twist bits have shanks for 1/4" drills but drill 5/16", 3/8", 7/16", and 1/2" holes. Because they tend to overload the drill, first make a smaller lead hole in metal or hard wood. Let the drill cool if it heats.

A countersink bit drills a hole for a screwhead to sink into. The one shown at right drills both wood and metal. Countersinks usually work best at slow speeds.

Long-shanked twist bits, many about 6" long, are available in 1/4" diameter or smaller. Use one only where you need an extra long bit.

A pilot bit, available in many sizes, will drill the proper lead hole for a screw's threads, a larger hole for its shank, and countersink a hole for its head — all in one operation.

Masonry bits are tipped with tungsten carbide to chew slowly through concrete and stone, somewhat faster through mortar joints and brick. Large ones require considerable power; a 1/2" bit with reduced shank is the largest for a 1/4" drill. For information on drilling with these, see page 51.

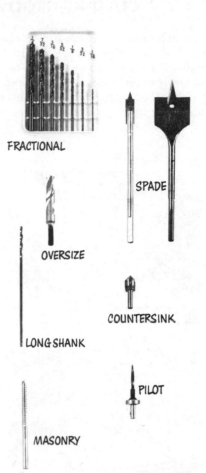

FRACTIONAL

SPADE

OVERSIZE

COUNTERSINK

LONG SHANK

PILOT

MASONRY

Hole saw *cuts several sizes of holes.*

Screwdrivers *for drills are handy.*

Disc sander *smoothes wood quickly. The disc attaches to shaft with a ball joint, allowing disc to lie flat.*

Electric chisel, *fitting into a drill, chews grooves in very soft woods. Both 1/2" and 3/4" sizes are made.*

Drill press *positions a hand-held power drill for drilling holes straight. Some fit particular drills; others adapt for all.*

CUTTING GROOVES WITH CHISELS

A chisel is most commonly used for cutting grooves and mortises. Some mortises, like those needed for recessing hinge leaves, are quite shallow, whereas others, like those in mortise-and-tenon joinery, may be quite deep.

Chisels often come in sets; a typical set of four standard chisels is shown at right. This type, equipped with metal-capped plastic handles, is handy for cutting small grooves and notches. You may not need a complete set of four (¼", ½", ¾", and 1"); buy them as you need them.

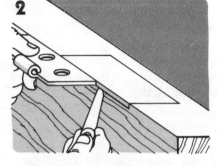

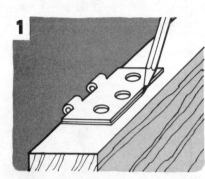

1 Outline with a pencil the area to be removed. If mortising for a hinge, use the hinge as a template.

2 Score along the lines with a sharp tool. If the mortise will be open on one side, score the depth as well.

3 Lightly rap the chisel on each cross-grain mark (bevel facing waste wood) to keep the mortise from splitting beyond those marks.

4 Moving with the blade's bevel forward, make a series of parallel cuts to the desired depth. The chisel should be almost vertical to the surface.

5 Chip out all the waste wood that has been loosened, hand holding the chisel and decreasing its angle considerably.

6 Working from one side, make final smoothing cuts with the chisel almost flat. If mortising a hinge, check it for uniformly flush fit.

A For a deeper mortise, first make a series of holes with a drill to remove most of the excess wood.

B Then join the series of holes and square-up the resulting mortise, using a chisel.

USING PLANES PROPERLY

A plane slices off unwanted portions of wood, controlling a cut's width and depth. Several varieties are available. You should be familiar with two main categories: block and bench planes.

The small block plane, held in one hand, is used for shaving down rounded surfaces, planing a board's end grain, and on-the-spot smoothing.

A bench plane shaves in the direction of the wood grain. The fore, jack, and smooth planes, all in the bench plane category, are differentiated by length. The shortest (smooth plane) rides up and down irregularities; the longest (fore plane) glides across a surface, knocking off high spots. The jack plane is a useful compromise.

Before using a plane, check the blade edge's angle and exposure by sighting down the plane's underside. The edge should protrude very slightly through the slot and should be square. Bench planes are adjusted by pushing a lateral adjustment lever toward the extended corner of the blade. With a block plane, release the blade-clamping device ("cam cap") and adjust it by hand. A bench plane's blade is mounted bevel down; a block plane's is bevel up.

Hold a block plane in one hand, applying pressure to the front knob with the forefinger. Cut end grain with short, shearing strokes. To prevent splitting a board's edge when planing end grain, either plane inward, slightly bevel the edge first, or clamp a piece of scrap wood to the edge, planing scrap and the board's edge together.

A bench plane cuts best in a slightly angled shearing motion. Keep cuts shallow and even, applying most force on the front knob at the beginning of a stroke, evening out pressure at the middle, and finally applying force to the handle at the stroke's end.

For more specialized cabinet joinery, special-duty planes are made for jobs like routing, grooving, and chamfering.

THE ELECTRIC ROUTER

One very sophisticated power tool that performs as an electric chisel, wood-carving knife, and plane is the router. This expensive tool is excellent for cabinetmaking. It cuts all kinds of grooves: dadoes (see page 26), V-grooves, rounded grooves, and even exact dovetails. It can round or bevel the edge of a board or finish the edge of plastic laminate at a single pass. Used with the proper cutter and template, it can whisk out hinge mortises in minutes.

Because it is a powerful, high-speed cutting tool, the router requires careful set-up and practice. Using one properly can be demanding; be sure to follow manufacturer's instructions and recommendations.

ABRASIVE TOOLS (FILES & RASPS)

Abrasive tools, such as files and rasps, are used for removing small quantities of a material or smoothing small areas. Some types abrade metals; others are strictly for wood. The material they cut depends upon the fineness and closeness of their rows of teeth. Very fine teeth are usually meant for filing metal and smoothing wood. Coarser "rasps" are designed for rapidly abrading wood. Perforated metal rasps come in several shapes and sizes and with replaceable blades. They are meant for abrading wood, soft metals, and plastics. They are particularly good for planing end grain and convex surfaces.

Buy files and rasps as you need them. A few of the main types you may find useful are shown. Sandpaper is discussed on page 55.

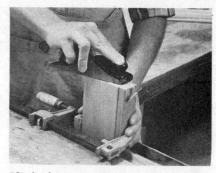
Block plane *cuts end grain well. Notice the scrap block clamped to board's edge to keep it from splitting.*

Jack plane *shears bumps and irregularities off. Always cut in line with the grain, keeping even pressure on the plane.*

Router *grooves, shaves, bevels, and rounds wood, depending upon the bit.*

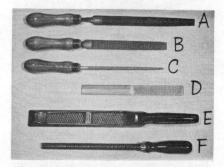
Files and rasps *shown:* **(A)** *10″ half-round file,* **(B)** *8″ half-round rasp,* **(C)** *8″ round file,* **(D)** *10″ shoe rasp,* **(E)** *flat perforated rasp,* **(F)** *round perforated rasp.*

Assembling materials

Materials must be fastened together to form a finished project. Although fasteners, like nails and screws, play an important role in joinery, the way the wooden pieces fit together is equally important; when two pieces are simply butted together and fastened, the resulting joint is not as strong as when two pieces are cut to interlock. The more both pieces interlock and the larger the surface area of contact, the stronger the joint will be.

Several joinery options exist that involve different joinery techniques and kinds of fasteners. A discussion of these follows. To choose the right joints and fasteners, you'll need to decide upon the required strength, the appearance you wish the project to have, and the work you are willing to do. One word of advice: unless you revel in hewing hard-to-make joints, don't try to make joints more complicated than your skills and tools will allow — you may exhaust your share of time and patience before the project is finished. Just be sure the joint is strong enough to do the job. Most projects in this book favor simple joinery. In almost all cases, experienced woodworkers can substitute more sophisticated joints.

FORMING WOODEN JOINTS

Either hand or power tools can be used for cutting wood for joints. Hand tools are usually less expensive and easier to control; in experienced hands, power tools make a wider variety of cuts for joints faster and often more precisely.

All of the wooden joints on the facing page are made from three basic cuts: a simple through cut (a cut all the way through a board), a rabbet cut (two cuts at 90° angles to each other at a board's end), and a dado cut (a groove falling intermediately along a board). Some of these cuts are easy to make with either hand or power tools; others are not feasible without the help of power tools.

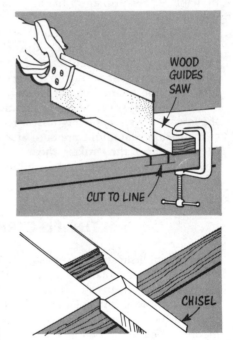

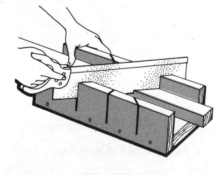

A through cut is made using the saws and methods discussed on pages 17-20. Easily controlled, fine-cutting saws are best for most joints. The backsaw and miter box shown are a sure bet for cutting narrow boards; equipped with fine-toothed blades, a table saw, radial-arm saw, and portable circular saw (used with a guide) are good for cutting larger stock. Accurately mark (page 15), then simply cut along the waste side of the line, leaving the line showing.

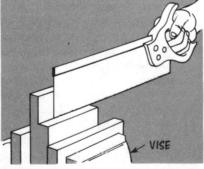

A rabbet cut is actually two cuts that meet each other at right angles at the end of a board. Mark the lines using a square; then use a saw to cut them (again, the more control, the better). A rabbet can also be cut by the same methods used for cutting dadoes; the only difference between a rabbet and a dado is that a rabbet is always at a board's end.

A dado cut is not as easy to make as the other cuts described, especially when you're using hand tools. The trick is to cut a wide groove with a flat base. The most popular tools for making narrow dadoes are routers and power saws equipped with special dado blades. Simply set the blade's depth guide and make one or more passes across the wood. Another way to cut a dado is to make several cuts within the dado's boundaries with a saw; then chisel out the waste wood. The section on chisels (page 24) shows how to cut mortises (which are, in essence, dadoes); that section also shows the principle of initially using a drill to remove waste wood from a very deep mortise. One other commonly-available tool fits in a power drill and cuts grooves to about 1" deep (see page 23).

WOOD JOINERY METHODS

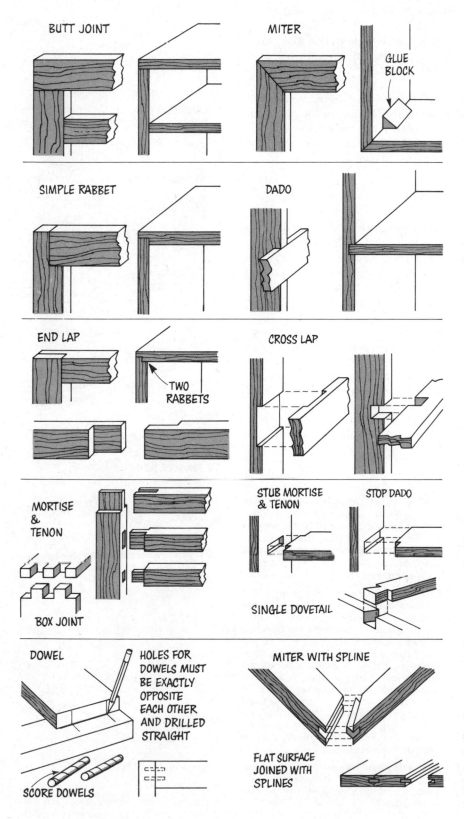

Butt joints and miters are the easiest joints to make; you just saw through the pieces and fit them together. Both kinds are weak; they require fastening with glue, glue blocks, nails, screws, bolts, dowels, or splines (see bottom of page).

The simple rabbet (far left) is stronger and shows less end grain than a butt joint. Secure it with glue and fasteners.

A dado, near left, is a strong way to inset a support or hold a shelf. Glue alone will hold some dadoes.

End laps and cabinet corner joint at far left are made from two corresponding rabbets, cut at the end of joining pieces. The cuts in the rails are easily made with a handsaw; those across the broader surfaces may require a power saw. Although rabbeted joints are stronger than butt joints and miters, they need to be strengthened with glue and sometimes with fasteners.

Cross lap joints (near left) are made by cutting matching dadoes in two pieces. Some don't need glue or fasteners; they are ideal where you want to dismantle joints.

Mortise and tenon variations (far left) are made by cutting (sometimes quite deeply) a dado in one piece to interlock with a mortise at the end of another. Cutting the mortise is similar to cutting a multiple rabbet. A box joint is like several open mortises and tenons. The stop dado and stub mortise and tenon, near left, both will hold a shelf without exposing the dado groove. The single dovetail is a lock-type joint.

Dowels (far left) make simple joints strong. All you do is drill holes for the dowels in each piece (special "dowel centers" are available for centering the dowels in both halves), cut the dowels to a size slightly shorter than the combined depth of matching holes, score small grooves along the dowels so glue can escape the holes, spread glue along each dowel, insert them, and clamp the joint tight.

A wooden spline, inserted in a saw kerf, is a sure and simple way to strengthen miters and butt joints. A spline's width should be slightly less than combined depth of kerfs. Glue and clamp.

GLUING THINGS TOGETHER

One of the best fasteners for a joint that you won't want to dismantle is glue. When used correctly, glue can usually make a joint as strong as the wood itself.

Gluing once was a messy and frustrating job. Although bottled glues have long been available, for years a heated pot of animal glue was the only sure solution for getting a reliable bond. Some materials couldn't be successfully bonded with anything.

Today, nearly all materials can be neatly and durably joined with adhesives. The only difficulty lies in selecting the right adhesive for the particular job and using it properly. Look through the following discussion and decide which glue is best for your project; then use it as directed on the label. The proper clamping of pieces often plays an important part in bonding; clamps are also discussed here.

Choosing glues

The trick to selecting the right glue is in matching the type of bond to the desired end result. Some glues set or cure to a hard, brittle state. Others, while setting to a rather stiff bond, remain slightly flexible. Still others stay soft and rubbery. It's not wise to choose a flexible adhesive for a cabinet joint, but for joining dissimilar materials, a flexible adhesive is often best. Dissimilar materials expand and contract at different rates, and a rigid bond will simply break away.

Another consideration in your choice of adhesive is the environment. For outdoor use or where humidity is high, select waterproof glue. In very dry areas, avoid adhesives that become brittle when dry.

Chemicals may also attack adhesives. Chemical-curing adhesives are generally resistant to most household chemicals, such as cleaning fluids, turpentine, paint thinner, and kerosene. Moisture-sensitive adhesives usually break down immediately when subjected to ammonia or strong detergents. Here are the common types of adhesives available in hardware and variety stores:

Animal glue. Also called "hide glue," this is the oldest type of wood glue. It may be applied as hot or cold liquid, is strong, and is often used in building furniture. However, animal glue does have poor resistance to moisture and tends to become brittle with age. It is often used to join veneers of wood. Clamp glued surfaces until dry.

Casein glue. Usually found in a powdered form ready to be mixed with water, this adhesive has fairly good strength and better moisture resistance than animal glue. It is made from milk protein. Because it is nontoxic, casein glue is often used in toy construction. It requires a thin application and sets slowly. Clamp glued surfaces until dry.

Contact cement. Handy for bonding surfaces that can't be clamped, contact cement forms a permanent bond on contact. It is usually used for such jobs as applying countertop plastic or plywood edging. It is generally applied with an old brush or roller. Because the bond formed is permanent, prefit all surfaces before applying cement. Once cement has dried on each surface, carefully align parts and push them together. Doing this part takes the most care, for once the two surfaces touch, they won't budge. (For more on laying plastic with contact cement, see page 13.)

Epoxy. This glue consists of a resin and a curing agent that must be measured and mixed together. Because it cures chemically, it is excellent for bonding nonporous materials. It forms a strong bond and is available in a slightly flexible form. Although good for bonding a large number of materials, it will dissolve some plastics. Epoxy sets at a lower temperature than other glues and in wet conditions. You need not clamp joints being glued. Never use epoxy on a joint that may later require dismantling or adjustment.

Hot-melt glue. This synthetic resin adhesive is purchased in sticks that are used in electric glue guns. Easy to use, it sets quickly. It cannot be adjusted once dry and has only moderate

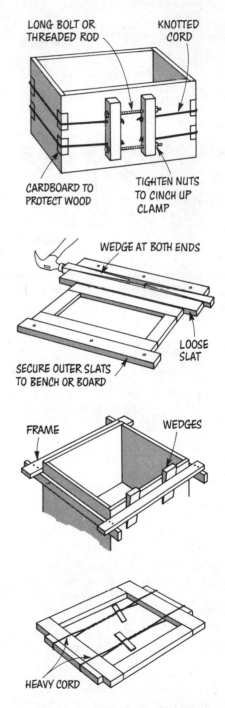

LONG BOLT OR THREADED ROD

KNOTTED CORD

CARDBOARD TO PROTECT WOOD

TIGHTEN NUTS TO CINCH UP CLAMP

WEDGE AT BOTH ENDS

LOOSE SLAT

SECURE OUTER SLATS TO BENCH OR BOARD

FRAME

WEDGES

HEAVY CORD

Homemade clamping devices *are easy to make using scrap wood and materials.*

strength and durability. Clamp glued surfaces until glue sets.

Resorcinol resin. A two-part adhesive, resorcinol resin cures chemically. The bond it forms is very strong and remains slightly flexible when cured. This flexibility and a resistance to moisture make it a good choice for use on outdoor construction or indoors around moisture. The liquid resin is flammable and sometimes leaves a dark line when it dries. Clamp surfaces until glue sets.

Urea-formaldehyde glue. Also called a "urea-resin" adhesive, this glue comes in dry powder to be mixed with water. Keep both casein and urea glues in tightly sealed containers because even the moisture in the air can make the powders lumpy and crusty. Urea glue has good strength and heat resistance, but it is not recommended for outdoor use. Don't use it in poorly fitted joints because it loses its strength when applied too thickly. It is most commonly used in making furniture, veneering, and joining large wooden surfaces.

White glue (polyvinyl acetate). White glue is the milky-white liquid most often found in plastic squeeze bottles. Although called "white" glue, it dries by loss of water to a semi-clear glue line. White glue has only moderate moisture resistance and strength. But it does have good resistance to grease and solvents and is fine for gluing wood. Glued surfaces should be clamped until dry. Wipe off excess; most stains and transparent finishes will not take to glue-coated areas.

Using clamps

Having a few good clamps available can be more helpful than having an extra pair of hands. Not only can clamps exert extreme pressure on pieces being glued, but also they can hold a piece of lumber on a workbench, enabling you to work with both hands. Shown in the photograph below are a few of the major commercial clamps. Buy them as you need them.

A carpenter's tip: to protect wood surfaces from being marred by the jaws of a metal clamp, slip a scrap block between the jaws and the wood surface before tightening the clamp.

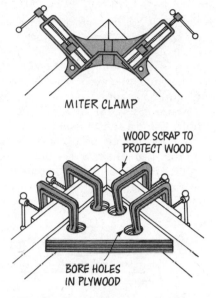

MITER CLAMP

WOOD SCRAP TO PROTECT WOOD

BORE HOLES IN PLYWOOD

Clamping miters *is easy by using a special clamp made for the purpose, or by making your own clamp.*

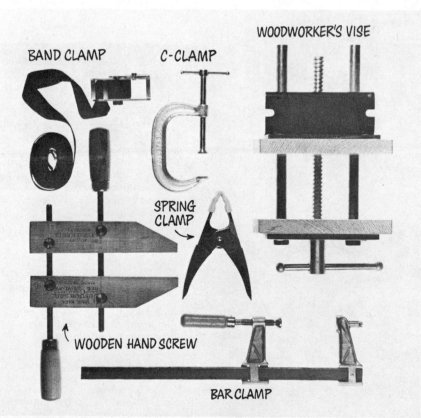

BAND CLAMP C-CLAMP WOODWORKER'S VISE

SPRING CLAMP

WOODEN HAND SCREW

BAR CLAMP

Band clamp is used for clamping unusually-shaped pieces together. You simply wrap a canvas strap loop around the pieces and tightly draw it into a metal buckle.

C-clamp is handy and inexpensive. It clamps materials together or to a workbench. Basic jaw widths are available from 3" to 16".

Woodworker's vise bolts to a workbench or sawhorse, holding materials securely and freeing both your hands for work. Large jaws evenly distribute pressure. Most vises come without hardwood faces, you add the wood. When bench-mounting a vise, keep top of jaws flush with bench top.

Spring clamp is used for clamping light materials. Like a large clothespin, two spring-loaded handles keep jaws tight until they are squeezed together.

Wooden hand-screw adjusts for both angle and distance, making irregular, flat-sided objects easy to clamp. Keep jaws parallel to surfaces being clamped.

Bar clamp, like the larger pipe clamp, is excellent for clamping face frames and clamping across broad materials. Because of its quick adjustability, a short bar clamp like the one shown is very handy for miscellaneous clamping.

NAILING — FAST & EASY

Although nailing is neither the strongest nor the most attractive fastening method, it is easy, inexpensive, and fast. Once you've mastered nail terminology and understood the differences between the many kinds, you'll be well on your way to using them correctly.

Nails. Nails are made for all kinds of jobs. Among the more usual varieties are "common," "box," "casing," and "finish" nails. These are shown at right. You've probably used either common or box nails many times; they resemble each other, but the box nail is thinner. Although it is less likely to split wood, the box nail bends more easily. Because they have heads, common and box nails have more holding power than finish or casing nails.

Choose casing or finish nails for jobs where you don't want nail heads visible. Using a nailset, you can knock these practically headless nails below the surface, leaving only a small hole to fill. The finish nail, slightly thinner than the casing nail, works best in hardwoods.

All four kinds of nails come in sizes ranging from 2-penny to 16-penny; you can usually find the common nail in sizes up to 60-penny. What's a

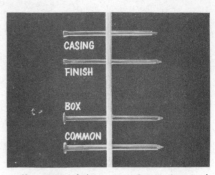

Nails are quick fasteners. Set casing and finish nails below surface; use box and common nails for strength.

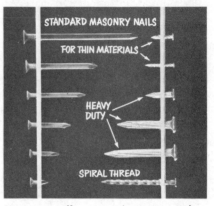

Masonry nails come in many styles. Wear eye protection when driving them.

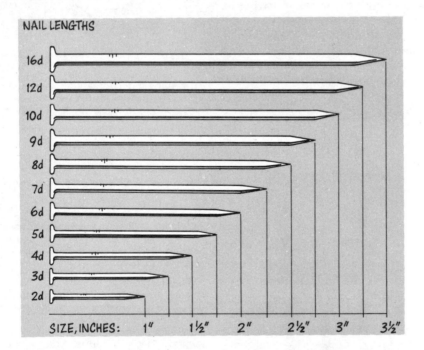

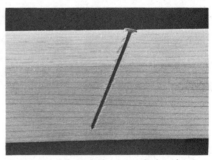

Grip wood better with nails by driving them in at a slight angle.

Far left. Corrugated fasteners (bottom in photo) and scotch screws (top left) join wood quickly. Corrugated fasteners, by far the strongest, can be driven easily with the special tool shown.

Near left. Brads (right of hammer) and special tacks and staples (left of hammer) are just a few of many small fasteners available. The tack hammer simplifies driving most kinds.

penny? Long ago the term "penny" (abbreviated as "d") meant the cost of a hundred hand-forged nails; a hundred of the smallest nails, for example, sold for two pennies. Now the term indicates a nail's length. Equations in inches are given in the chart on the facing page.

Choosing the proper nail length for a particular job is very important. Although the nail should not poke out the backside of materials being fastened, it should be long enough to hold firmly. For strongest nailing, choose a nail three times longer than the top thickness being fastened. (For example, use a 1½" nail when nailing ½" plywood to a 2 by 4.) Don't choose a nail that is shorter than twice the top material's thickness. (When possible, nail from the thinnest material to the thickest.)

Although steel nails are the most common, aluminum and bronze nails are made for more specialized work. Specify hot-dipped, galvanized nails when they will be subject to moisture.

Masonry nails, available in a wide range of sizes, can be driven into curing concrete, concrete block, soft stone, mortar, and brick. When pounded into seasoned concrete or hard stone, these high-carbon nails tend to chip out the material and then, though they maintain lateral holding power, won't hold against an outward pull. When hanging something on a hard masonry wall, use masonry anchors (see page 50). Always wear eye protection when driving masonry nails. Start the nail straight, hitting squarely with light "one-two" strokes. Don't hit them hard or drive them further than ¾" into masonry.

Other common hammer-driven fasteners (shown on the facing page) include corrugated fasteners, tacks, staples, and decorative nails and pins.

Hammers. To drive a nail you need a hammer. Pick one that is the right weight for you — a 14 or 16-ounce head is popular. Be sure the hammer has a curved claw (not a straight claw) and a smooth face (the part that hits the nail) that is slightly rounded in profile. Choose one that is made from high-tempered steel.

Nailing technique. Nails with sharp points hold better than blunt ones but tend to split the wood. Blunt the point with a tap of the hammer before driving into wood that splits easily. And don't line up two nails along the same grain lines in the board — you'll split the wood if you do. Instead, stagger nails slightly, as shown at right.

When starting a nail, hold it near its head between your thumb and forefinger and give it a few light taps. If you miss when holding it this way, you'll only knock your fingers away instead of smashing them. Once the nail is started, take your fingers away and swing the hammer with fuller strokes, hitting the nail squarely. Visualize a pivot point at the handle's end and keep that point level with the nailhead. Where you wish to maintain a handsome wood finish, don't crush the wood with the last few hammer blows. Using a nailset, set the heads of finish or casing nails about 1/16" below the surface to hide them from view.

Pull out a nail by wedging the claw around the nail's shank, under its head, and rocking the hammer backward. Guard against marring the wood by placing a flat stick between hammerhead and surface. Use a thicker block and rock the hammer sideways to add leverage for balky or long nails. Doing this will keep the nail's hole small and prevent the hammer handle from breaking.

STAPLING — ONE-HANDED FASTENING

Lightweight staplers, such as the one shown, are handy for jobs requiring many short fasteners (for example, fastening a thin back onto a cabinet). Using a stapler is easier than driving a small nail because you can squeeze the stapler with one hand while holding the material with the other.

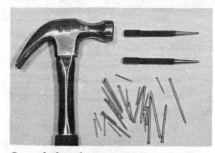

Curved-claw hammer and *nailsets are common to cabinetmaking. Several sizes of nailsets are available.*

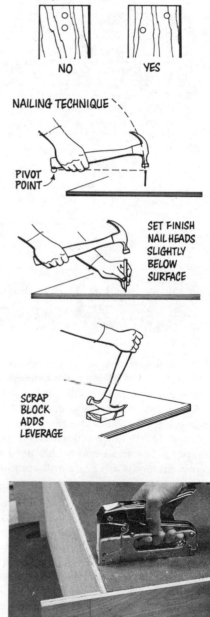

PROPER NAIL PLACEMENT

NO   YES

NAILING TECHNIQUE

PIVOT POINT

SET FINISH NAIL HEADS SLIGHTLY BELOW SURFACE

SCRAP BLOCK ADDS LEVERAGE

Stapler, *a one-handed tool, shoots small staples through thin materials.*

DRIVING SCREWS PROPERLY

Although screws are slightly more difficult and time consuming to drive than nails, they are considerably stronger, especially when supplemented with glue. Used without glue, they can be removed, creating a demountable joint.

Buying screws. Screws are classified by gauge (thickness), length, head type, and metallic make-up. As shown in the chart, each gauge includes a variety of lengths. Common screws run up to 6″ in length; square-headed lag screws come in diameters from ¼″ to 1″; lengths from 1½″ to 12″.

When possible, plan to screw through the thinnest material into the thickest. For a strong joint, choose a screw three times longer than (and not less than twice as long as) the thickness of the top piece being fastened.

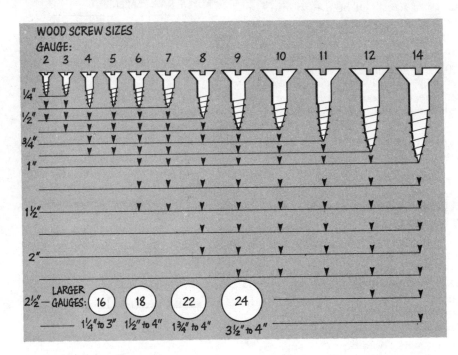

If the two surfaces being joined are of equal thickness, be sure the screw isn't so long that it will poke through. A good rule of thumb: the unthreaded shank of the screw should just penetrate the top board.

Screw heads may be round (sit above the surface); flat (countersunk below surface); oval and pan (more decorative, above the surface); Phillips (slotted for Phillips screwdriver); and lag (square-headed, driven with a wrench). The most commonly used screws are made of steel; other softer screw materials are brass and aluminum.

Screwdrivers. Most people are familiar with the ordinary screwdriver, but many don't know how to use it properly. If a screwdriver is too large or small for a screw's slot, it can easily burr the screwhead or slip off, gouging the work. You'll probably need two or three sizes; purchase them as the need arises. In some situations, an ordinary driver won't work — you'll need several sizes of Phillips screwdrivers for driving various Phillips screws (they won't slip out of screwhead as easily as a slotted screwdriver in a slotted head).

A screwdriver-bit attachment for electric drills lessens the effort of driving a large number of screws (see page 23). If you own a variable-speed drill, a simple bit shaped like a screwdriver tip is all you need. Drills without variable speeds require a speed reducing, clutch-type mechanism.

Flathead screw *sits flush or countersinks below wood's surface.*

Roundhead screw *holds where top piece is too thin to countersink screwhead.*

Ovalhead screw *countersinks part way; rounded top sits above surface.*

Phillips heads *keep driver centered.*

Sheet-metal screw *is strong in wood.*

Lag screw *is powerfully strong; you must drive it with a wrench.*

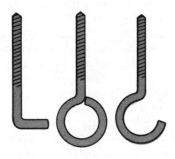

Screw hooks *and eyes can hang objects.*

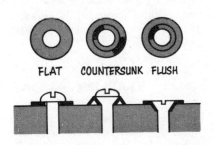

Washers *for screws come in three styles.*

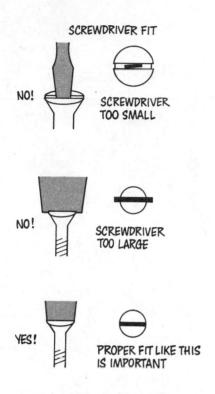

SCREWDRIVER FIT

NO! — SCREWDRIVER TOO SMALL

NO! — SCREWDRIVER TOO LARGE

YES! — PROPER FIT LIKE THIS IS IMPORTANT

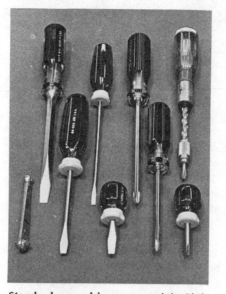

Standard screwdrivers are on left; Phillips drivers are on the right. Offset screwdriver (at lower left) and short screwdrivers (bottom) work in tight spots. Tool at upper right drives screws when you push down on it.

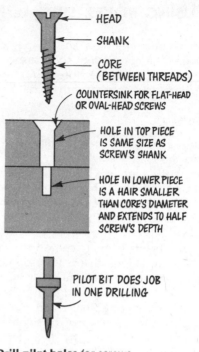

HEAD

SHANK

CORE (BETWEEN THREADS)

COUNTERSINK FOR FLAT-HEAD OR OVAL-HEAD SCREWS

HOLE IN TOP PIECE IS SAME SIZE AS SCREW'S SHANK

HOLE IN LOWER PIECE IS A HAIR SMALLER THAN CORE'S DIAMETER AND EXTENDS TO HALF SCREW'S DEPTH

PILOT BIT DOES JOB IN ONE DRILLING

Drill pilot holes for screws.

Installing screws. Sometimes screws refuse to be driven. When the going gets rough, the screw's head usually gets ruined. A cheaply made, burred, bent, or improperly sized driver may be the problem. Or perhaps you may not be installing the screws correctly.

In all but the very softest wood, you should drill holes before driving in regular or long screws. When using small, short screws in soft woods, drilling a hole is unnecessary — provide a starting hole using an awl or punch (page 21). Mark the screw's position on the top board, then drill a hole the same size as the screw's shank. For flathead or ovalhead screws, countersink a hole that matches the head's diameter. Position the top board on the lower board and drill a pilot hole for the threaded portion of the screw. This hole should reach about half the length of the screw, and its diameter should be a hair smaller than the core between the threads. To make drilling screw holes easy, buy a special "pilot bit" that drills different size holes for the thread, shank, and head of a screw, all at the same time. Some pilot bits are adjustable; others you buy in sets that match screw sizes.

If a screwdriver still requires undue muscle and burrs the screw's slot when the screw is only partially in, remove and discard the screw and enlarge the lead hole for another. When driving brass or aluminum screws (especially long ones in hard woods), it helps to drive in and remove a similar size steel screw first, forming threads for the softer metal screws. Rubbing a bit of soap or wax on a screw's threads also makes it easier to drive. Be sure to keep the screwdriver straight and squarely seated in the screw's slot.

For fine-finish cabinetwork, countersink flathead screws below the wood's surface; then fill the hole above the head with putty or a wooden plug. To plug a screw hole in a fine surface, don't use doweling — the grain runs the wrong direction. Instead, use a plug of the same type of wood, cutting it with a "plug-cutter bit" (made for electric drills — a drill press works best).

To use a lag screw, drill a hole two-thirds its diameter and length, start it with a hammer, and drive it tight with a wrench. Lag-threaded hooks and eyes (used for hanging objects) are installed the same way. You can use a stick, rod, screwdriver, or similar lever to turn them tight.

To hide a screw, countersink it well below the surface; then fill the hole with a wooden plug. Plug cutter, fitted in an electric drill, cuts the plug from the same type wood so plug matches.

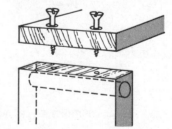

INSERT A DOWEL WHEN SCREWING INTO END GRAIN

USING BOLTS, SPECIAL FASTENERS, AND BRACKETS

Many different sizes and shapes of bolts, special fasteners, and joinery brackets are available; some are common, others are not. Browse through your local hardware store to find out what is readily available to you.

Here are some facts that you'll need to know about bolts:

Bolts

Unlike pointed screws, bolts have threaded shafts that receive nuts. To use them, drill a hole, push the bolt through, and add a nut. Because they are not dependent upon the threads' ability to grip wood, bolts are very strong and don't chew up the wood when removed.

Bolts are made from steel (carbon, stainless, and zinc-plated), titanium, bronze, brass, and aluminum. Zinc-plated steel bolts are most commonly used.

The heads of bolts come in several shapes. Consider two factors when choosing among them: their appearance (if they will be visible) and the tools necessary for tightening them. You'll need screwdrivers (regular or Phillips) for slotted-head bolts, wrenches or pliers for hex or square-headed bolts and nuts. Carriage and ribbed bolts have self-anchoring heads that dig into the wood when you tighten the nut.

Bolts are classified by diameter and number of threads per inch; a ⅜" by 20 bolt is ⅜" in diameter and has 20 threads to the inch. Common bolts sizes run from ⅛" by 40 to ½" by 13, but hex and square-head machine bolts have diameters up to 2" (large sizes must usually be special ordered). Lengths run from ⅜" to 30". The longer bolts are not normally stocked in hardware stores. If you can't find one long enough, use threaded rod, discussed on the facing page.

Choose a bolt that's as long as the thicknesses being fastened plus ½" (unless you countersink the nut in a shallowly drilled hole). Drill a hole

SCREW'S THREADS MUST GRIP WOOD

BOLT THREADS DON'T GRIP WOOD, BUT YOU NEED ACCESS TO THIS SIDE

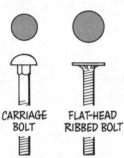

CARRIAGE BOLT   FLAT-HEAD RIBBED BOLT

THESE BOLTS HAVE SELF-ANCHORING HEADS

SQUARE-HEAD BOLT   HEXAGON-HEAD BOLT

BOLT HEADS YOU HOLD WITH A WRENCH

YOU TIGHTEN THESE BOLTS WITH A SCREWDRIVER, HOLDING THE NUT WITH A WRENCH

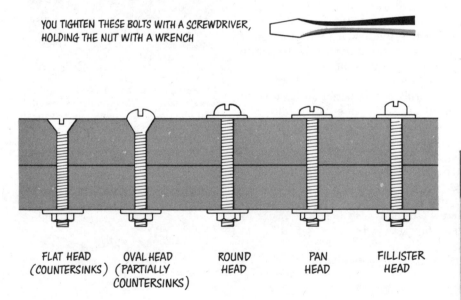

FLAT HEAD (COUNTERSINKS)   OVAL HEAD (PARTIALLY COUNTERSINKS)   ROUND HEAD   PAN HEAD   FILLISTER HEAD

(ALL OF THESE STYLES ALSO AVAILABLE WITH PHILLIPS HEADS)

Countersink bolt heads the same way you'd countersink a screw (previous page). A dowel will work, but a plug cutter cuts a plug with proper grain.

1/16" larger than the bolt's diameter unless it needs a snug fit. Place washers under the head and nut of all but the self-anchoring or countersinking bolts; for those, put a washer under the nut only.

Nuts and washers

Hexagonal and square-shaped nuts and round washers are most often used in woodworking, but, as you can see in the illustration, options are available. Special-purpose nuts include wing nuts, knurled nuts, acorn nuts, and T-nuts. Wing and knurled nuts can be quickly tightened and removed by hand. Acorn nuts decoratively cap the ends of bolts. T-nuts, fitting flush on a surface, provide metal threads in a hole. A T-nut is strong only when pulled from the side of the hole opposite its body. It cannot withstand a pull from the same side.

Special fasteners

Other fasteners having bolt-like threads include threaded rod, eyes and hooks, hanger bolts, U-bolts, and binding screws.

Threaded rod ("all thread") can be cut to any length using a hacksaw. It is available in standard lengths of 2', 3', 6', and 12' and in diameters from ¼" to 1". Zinc-plated steel is most common; plain steel, stainless steel, and brass are available in some places. Use threaded rod as you would a bolt, but put washers and nuts at both ends.

Hook and eye bolts hang fixtures but can only be used when you have the necessary access for adding washers and nuts (see screw-threaded hooks and eyes on page 32). Hook and eye bolts, like other machine-threaded bolts, can be exchanged for the machine screws inserted in hollow-wall anchors (page 51). Diameters run from about ¼" to 2", lengths from 1" to 4".

Hanger bolts, when screwed or bolted to one surface, leave a threaded stud poking out. They are designed for hanging fixtures from walls. A fixture (such as a cabinet) is placed onto the stud, and a washer and nut are added. You can remove the fixture simply by removing the washers and nuts, saving the wall and fixture from being chewed up through insertion and removal of screws. Common lengths run from 2" to 6"; diameters are ¼", 5/16", and ⅜".

U-bolts usually attach flat surfaces (for instance, cabinet sides) to round poles or pipes. They are also the strongest fastener for hanging fixtures. Although they do the job of eye bolts, they provide twice the strength because they have two threaded shanks instead of one. Their sizing is complex; many sizes are available.

Binding screws join two surfaces and are demountable. You drill a hole large enough for the sleeve through both surfaces, insert the sleeve from one side, and screw the bolt into it from the other side. (Binding screws work much like T-nuts.) Lengths run from ¼" to 4".

Joinery brackets

Various "mending plates" and brackets are available which form strong joints alone and even stronger joints when used to supplement glued joints. Most are bright, zinc-plated steel, but some — those meant for decorative use — are brass or brass plated. The steel ones are generally meant to be hidden from view; the brass type, when visible, give projects a "campaign chest" look. The most common shapes are illustrated. L-shaped brackets are particularly useful for fastening rails or cabinet sides at right angles to each other or for fastening shelving systems to walls and ceilings (though they aren't made to support shelves from walls).

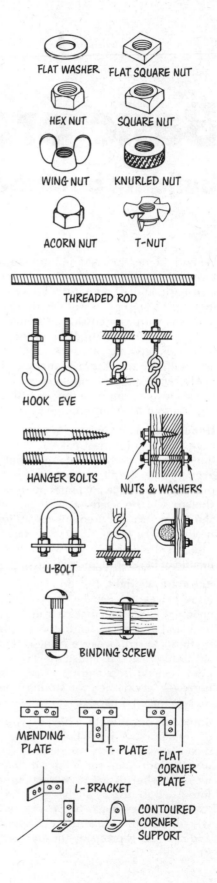

FLAT WASHER   FLAT SQUARE NUT
HEX NUT   SQUARE NUT
WING NUT   KNURLED NUT
ACORN NUT   T-NUT

THREADED ROD

HOOK   EYE

HANGER BOLTS   NUTS & WASHERS

U-BOLT

BINDING SCREW

MENDING PLATE   T-PLATE   FLAT CORNER PLATE
L-BRACKET   CONTOURED CORNER SUPPORT

Basic procedures
Building bookshelves & cabinets

When it comes to building bookshelves and cabinets, knowing how to use tools isn't quite enough. Order is important. You need to know how to turn basic know-how into building something specific. This section shows the step-by-step processes necessary for building bookshelves and cabinets. It begins with a discussion of simple shelving and then leads you through making basic cabinets, hanging doors, making drawers, and undertaking other cabinetwork; offers information on attaching completed units to walls and ceilings; and discusses methods for applying finishes.

Although this isn't a book on design theory, fundamental design principles can serve as a primer for the construction of bookshelves and cabinets, helping you to modify or redesign projects.

Dimensions are an important part of design. If a project is to succeed, it must have dimensions that make it workable and easy to use. Some average dimensions are shown at right, but modify these if your family isn't of average size. Don't place a shelf out of reach, make drawers too large to pull open, or place a counter at an uncomfortable height. Think about how shelves will be used—a shelf holding a set of encyclopedias should be shorter or stronger than one meant for holding paperback books; otherwise it will bow or break (see facing page). Be sure to check dimensions ahead: rueful is the woodworker who builds a large project in a shop and is later unable to fit it through the doorway.

Rules are all right, but don't feel you must follow convention. Although bookshelves are usually level from side to side and front to back, they needn't be. You can make a trough-style book holder by slanting the shelves back and adding a back to them. This makes an excellent holder for books of the same size because it keeps them uniformly seated. When shelves are slanted from end to end, a shelving unit takes on dynamic visual interest and doesn't need bookends. You can also leave the shelves level and tilt the books—a good trick for storing books in a hallway bookcase where the shelves must be narrow.

Bookshelf or cabinet—which do you need? This question is mostly a matter of semantics. A bookshelf is quite simple—usually just a surface with a means of support. A cabinet is a bit more complex—it has sides, a back, usually doors, and sometimes drawers or interior shelves. Generally speaking, bookshelves are considerably easier to make than cabinets. If you're interested in display shelving, perhaps a bookshelf is best. But if you'd like to store things out of view, your storage unit will need doors. For those who'd like both shelving and display areas, a wall system with both shelves and cabinets is probably the answer.

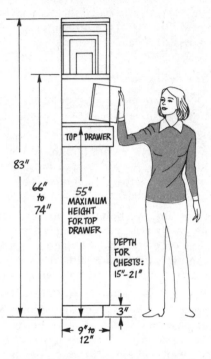

Proper dimensions *are important for making shelves and cabinets easy to use.*

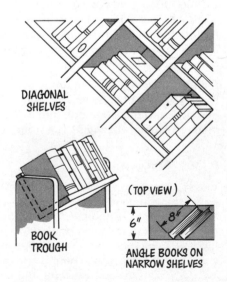

Try a new slant *on the ways you set books on shelves. Here are three ideas.*

Bookshelf basics

One of the easiest ways to make a bookshelf is to bridge a few large blocks with a board. After all, a shelf is just a flat surface that's supported at a certain height. Hundreds of variations exist. Shelves can be permanent or adjustable, supported in cabinets or closets (page 45), freestanding, wall-mounted, or even suspended from the ceiling. Many kinds of bookshelves are used throughout the projects in this book (pay particular attention to pages 58-61). Here are a few things to think about when choosing a particular type of shelving:

Permanent or adjustable? Although each has its place, adjustable shelving is usually preferred to permanent—it helps eliminate waste space. Shelves can be made adjustable in many ways; some methods are shown on page 45; others are described in the projects. You can buy adjustable standards in lengths from 12" to 12' for wall-mounted shelves. For creative ways of utilizing shelving hardware see page 66.

Standing or hanging? Although freestanding bookcases can be rearranged with the furniture and some can have additional roles as room dividers, they must supply all the necessary structure for supporting shelves and require more materials than bookcases using walls or ceilings for support. Shelves hung from the ceiling require only a handful of hooks and a couple of lengths of chain or rope; shelves fastened to a wall don't need a back. And a wall or ceiling-attached unit can free floor space beneath the shelves, unless shelves extend to the floor. For hanging shelves from ceilings or walls, you'll need firm fastening supports (see page 50). If you hesitate to put fasteners in walls, perhaps freestanding shelving or a unit wedged between ceiling and floor (see pressure devices, page 45) is best for you.

Shelf materials. Any rigid, flat material that supports the load set on it can be a shelf. Some typical shelf materials are lumber, plywood, particle board, hardboard, and glass (acrylic plastic sheet scratches too easily). These materials differ in cost, workability, appearance, rigidity, and durability.

Lumber (usually 1" or 2" thick by 8", 10", or 12" wide) is a favorite shelf material because it is rigid and easy to work—all you usually do is cut it to length. All materials but glass are available at most lumberyards. Glass (normally ¼" plate) can be purchased from a glass dealer. Tell him what you'll be using it for so he will grind the cut edges.

The proper thickness for a shelf material will depend upon its use and the amount of support given to it. A thick material requires less support than a thin one. The best way to determine how far a certain material will span and how much weight it will hold without bowing or breaking is to test it by supporting the ends with a couple of chairs and loading it with the weight it'll have to hold. If in doubt about the strength of a thickness, either choose a thicker material or add more support.

Tracks and brackets make shelves adjustable. Select permanent or adjustable shelving before choosing design.

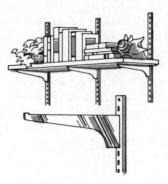

Hanging shelves are easy to make, require few materials. Standing bookcases are better for heavy loads.

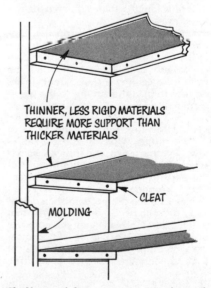

THINNER, LESS RIGID MATERIALS REQUIRE MORE SUPPORT THAN THICKER MATERIALS

CLEAT

MOLDING

Shelf materials can vary in size, depending upon the support given to them.

Building a simple cabinet

A simple cabinet can be made by turning a wooden box—a cabinet is basically a box—onto one of its sides. To make a more refined cabinet, though, you can construct the box yourself from attractive materials, later adding shelves (page 45), doors (pages 42-44), or drawers (pages 46-49).

Although cabinet construction methods vary, those used to make the cabinet shown at right are some of the most popular. The cabinet (also shown in the project on page 62) has exceptionally strong corner joints, a solidly-joined, handsome back, and well-hidden plywood edges. It has a pleasing appearance when given either a transparent or an opaque finish.

The cabinet's design has only one drawback: you need a table saw or similar power tool for precisely cutting the long rabbet grooves (see page 26). But don't give up if you don't own one of these power tools—alternative methods that are described can be used.

HERE'S HOW

Although the dimensions of the cabinet shown may differ from those you have in mind, they can serve as a handy reference point from which to work. Very large cabinets or those that will have drawers on center runners or double doors meeting at a "stile" should be built with a "face frame," (see page 40). Follow these six steps in constructing a cabinet:

1 Figure your cabinet's finished size. Don't neglect to consider the thickness of overlapping doors (page 42), if you plan to add them, and any other joinery alternatives that will affect the cutting dimensions. For example, if you don't inset the back, its thickness will add to the depth of the cabinet; butt-joined sides, top, and bottom will have different lengths than rabbeted or mitered ones.

Lay out the dimensions on the lumber. Plywood (¾") was chosen because of its resistance to warp—you may prefer to use solid lumber. If you'll be giving the cabinet a transparent finish, be sure to plan the cutting so the wood grain will run vertically along the pieces.

2 Cut the top, bottom, and sides to the proper width (if using a table-saw, set the fence and run all same-sized pieces through at one time). Cut the parts to the proper length; for rabbeted corners, sides should be ⅛" longer than the cabinet's finished height (a 3/16" allowance on each side that you'll later sand off) and the top and bottom pieces should be ¼" shorter than the cabinet's finished width (⅛" at each end for the rabbeted extension).

3 Cut the 5/16" by ⅝" rabbets along the back edges of all four pieces. The back panel will inset in these rab-

bets. Then cut the 13/16" by ⅝" rabbets at both ends of the side pieces. (See page 26 for information on cutting rabbets).

4 Spread glue along one of the side rabbets, join the bottom to it at right angles and flush at both back and front, and nail the two together with two or three 1½" finishing nails (setting the heads below the surface). Follow the same procedure for all four corners. It

helps to use long bar clamps (see page 29) to pull the pieces together before nailing, but clamps aren't essential.

5 Cut the ¼" plywood back to exact size so that it will be precisely "square"—90° at all corners. (The back will pull the entire cabinet into the proper shape.) If the back will be seen from behind, use A-A grade plywood; if it won't be seen, use A-D plywood, facing the good side into the cabinet (¼" hardboard also makes a good cabinet-back material). The back should fit snugly into the rabbeted grooves. Spread glue along the joint, put the

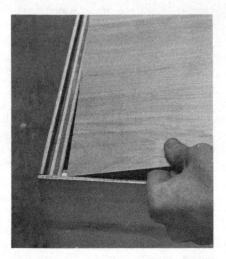

back in place, and nail it with 1" finishing nails, setting the heads slightly below the surface (if the back will be seen from behind).

6 Veneer tape disguises the edges of this plywood. It is available in several widths, wood types, and with or without adhesive backing. To apply the non-adhesive type, coat both the plywood edges and the veneer tape's back-

side with contact cement. Let the glue dry. Then, aligning one of the tape's edges with the cabinet's edge, carefully lay the tape in place. Press it down firmly and remove the excess with a razor blade or with sandpaper.

Fill nail holes and blemishes in the rest of the cabinet with putty; sand the entire unit. The cabinet is now ready for doors, shelves, or whatever additions you wish. Apply the finish after the unit is totally assembled.

ALTERNATIVES

In case you don't have the tools for building the cabinet as shown or just want to do it differently, here are some alternative construction methods.

Without power tools

It's possible to make a handsome cabinet without power tools. The job is nearly the same as the one described above, but you need to choose alternative techniques for joining the corners and back.

Making corner joints doesn't require cutting rabbets. A butt joint is by far the simplest way to join two surfaces.

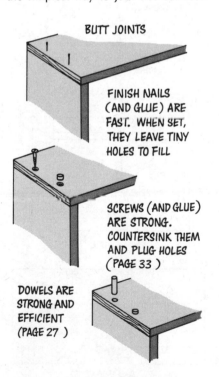

BUTT JOINTS

FINISH NAILS (AND GLUE) ARE FAST. WHEN SET, THEY LEAVE TINY HOLES TO FILL

SCREWS (AND GLUE) ARE STRONG. COUNTERSINK THEM AND PLUG HOLES (PAGE 33)

DOWELS ARE STRONG AND EFFICIENT (PAGE 27)

Just squirt glue along one piece, overlap the other piece, and nail, screw, or dowel the two together. If you nail, set the nailheads below the surface. Screws should be countersunk and plugged (see pages 32-33). If you use dowels, make them at least twice as

long as the outer surface's thickness. Cutting a shallow saw kerf just below the joint between the top and sides, as shown below, camouflages inaccuracies and adds visual interest.

For an extended-top cabinet, butt join two surfaces using the same methods, but extend the top further. When butt joining with plywood, the edge

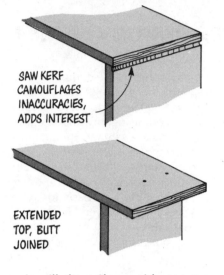

SAW KERF CAMOUFLAGES INACCURACIES, ADDS INTEREST

EXTENDED TOP, BUTT JOINED

grain will show. If you wish, you can use edging tape to cover the grain, just as you cover the cabinet's front edges.

Cabinetmakers often make cabinet corner joints by butting both surfaces to a solid piece of wood, hiding the plywood edges. The corner can then be rounded or tooled. If you do this, add corner brackets or glue blocks to the underside of the joint to strengthen the corners. Then glue and nail the solid piece into position, setting the nails.

SOLID CORNER

UNLESS SOLID CORNER IS SCREWED OR DOWELED IN PLACE, USE GLUE BLOCKS OR L-BRACKETS TO STRENGTHEN CORNER

FLUSH MOUNTED BACK IS NAILED TO CABINET'S BACK EDGE. INSET IT ⅛" AROUND ALL EDGES

INSET BACK BY FASTENING IT TO MOLDING

A THICKER FLUSH BACK CAN BE NAILED FROM AROUND PERIMETERS

Attaching the back is easy. Simply fasten the ¼" back to the back edges of the cabinet (you can inset it about ⅛" around all edges so it won't show from the front). If you don't want it visible from the sides, inset it by fastening it to blocks inside the cabinet. Or inset a ½" plywood back and nail it from around the cabinet's perimeter.

Using power tools

If the illustrated cabinet's rabbeted corner joints don't suit your purposes, one of these alternatives might. You'll need power tools to cut them.

DADO — STRONG, EASY TO CUT ON POWER SAW, CREATES EXTENDED CABINET TOP

MITER — LEAVES NO VISIBLE EDGE GRAIN, EASY TO CUT ON POWER SAW, IT IS DIFFICULT TO ASSEMBLE, AND WEAK

COMBINATION DADO MITER — STRONG VERSION OF MITER, BUT MORE DIFFICULT TO CUT

How to make a face-frame cabinet

A wooden frame attached to the face of a cabinet gives it strength, lateral stability, and the ability to accept lip-type doors (pages 42-43) and drawers on center runners (pages 46-48). Serving a function similar to that of a cabinet's back, a face frame joins cabinet pieces, adding rigidity and keeping the cabinet square (with 90° corners). All large or weak cabinets should have face frames.

The example constructed here—a bathroom vanity—illustrates the main points of building a basic face-frame cabinet. If you wish to make another kind of face-frame cabinet, you can use this example as a basis for your design. The vanity has double doors, drawers, a false drawer front, and a sink-bowl countertop. Options are also discussed.

Although not absolutely necessary, power tools can be very helpful in cutting and assembling the cabinet.

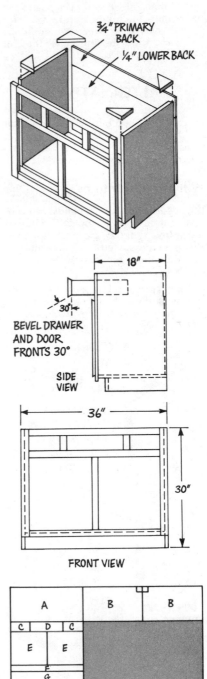

PLYWOOD LAYOUT
A: Bottom. B: Sides. C: Drawer fronts.
D: False drawer front. E: Doors.
F: Toe kick. G: Primary back. Make dimensions to suit. Use extra portion for back, drawers, shelves, etc.

HERE'S HOW

This cabinet's dimensions are given in the sketch; alter them if necessary to suit your cabinet. Decide whether your cabinet will have doors, drawers, a full or partial back, and what type of top it will have. If you plan to add a sink top, have it on hand for measurements.

Cut out the face-frame pieces, figuring their size by the cabinet's dimensions plus an additional 1/16" in all directions (the extra wood will be sanded flush after the cabinet is assembled).

1 Lay out the face-frame pieces, good face down, on a work surface and measure and mark them where they'll fit together. Work carefully, keeping all corners square.

2 Glue, clamp, and fasten the narrow top section of the frame. Be sure the pieces are good face down—you'll be using corrugated fasteners as shown. If you don't have bar or pipe clamps for cinching the pieces together, improvise with wedges as shown on page 28. Be sure all the pieces are flat against the work surface.

3 Keeping all pieces squarely aligned, assemble the rest of the frame in the same way (notice the clamp).

4 Use the assembled face frame to measure where to cut the plywood sides and bottom—remember to cut off a hair more of the plywood pieces so you can sand the face frame flush. Although grooves were cut into the sides for the back and the bottom, these cuts are not necessary—butt joining is almost as strong when gluing and nailing through the sides into the edges of 3/4" material. Cut the lower front corner of the sides for the "toe kick," as shown (if the cabinet will have one) into the sides. Keeping the pieces square, glue and nail them together (use 6d finish nails). You now have two sides and a bottom fastened together.

5 Spread glue around the edges of the cabinet and lay the face frame in place. Keeping everything square and leaving a slight, even overlap around all sides, nail the face frame to the plywood edges (use 6d finish nails).

6 Adding the back pulls the entire cabinet into square, so cut the back as square as possible. This cabinet has two backs: a short primary back of 3/4" plywood that will be fastened to the wall and a 1/4" plywood lower back that has cutouts for plumbing. Your cabinet's back will depend upon whether the cabinet will be wall-mounted or freestanding. Attach it using any of the methods shown on page 39. (Note: a hanging cabinet should have a 1/2" or 3/4" back that is nailed and glued very securely to the cabinet. Consider fastening it to cleats inside.)

7 Add a corner block to each of the four corners around the top edges; screw or glue the top to these corners once the vanity is in place. Because there is a sink in the center of this cabinet, the center hole at the front of the frame holds a false drawer front only. The other two small holes each hold a small drawer that slides on a center runner. Make the drawers (see pages 46-48). Because the drawer fronts and doors have beveled edges (30°), they don't require pulls. The doors work as lip doors, hiding inaccuracies of fit. (For more about hanging doors, see page 42.) Glue and nail the toe kick in place with 6d nails.

Set all nailheads, putty the holes, and stain or paint the cabinet. Fasten it to the wall through its back, using the methods explained on page 50.

Cabinet doors

Although cabinet doors can work several ways—hinge, slide, drop down, or roll away—all have the same duties of hiding clutter, enhancing a cabinet's appearance, and keeping the dust out. Drop-down doors also offer a work surface when open.

What type should you choose? Sliding doors are easy to install and always look tidy, but they only let you into half the cabinet at a time. The work involved in mounting hinged doors depends upon the hinges—some are easy to install; others are difficult. Hinged doors open easily and allow total access to a cabinet's contents, but they need room to swing. Drop-down doors are like hinged doors, but they swing down instead of to the side. Folding and tambour (roll-away) doors open the cabinet completely and require little or no swinging room, but are very difficult to make and install. For that reason, they are not discussed in this book.

Premade doors can also be purchased. A variety of facings and styles is available in standard sizes from builders' supply houses.

Although some cabinet doors are made from solid pieces of lumber joined together, most doors are made from panels of plywood, hardboard, or particle board (though particle board is quite heavy). Solid-lumber slab doors (made by doweling or splining together several lengths of lumber—see page 27) are hard to make, often too bulky and heavy, and tend to warp.

HINGED DOORS

Hundreds of styles of hinges exist, making it possible to hinge practically any door on any cabinet to give any appearance. You'll need to choose hinges that fit the cabinet and door, pivot properly, and look good on the finished piece. Some doors overlap the cabinet's edges; others sit inside between the edges. You'll need to consider the possibilities at right before choosing your hinges.

Most hinges come in packages of two, along with instructions for installation (some heavy doors require three hinges). Because butt hinges are often sold unpackaged, instructions for installing them are included on the facing page. (Turn the page for more about doors.)

Hinged doors are of three types: flush, overlapping, and offset (lip). Flush doors amplify fitting errors; when the cabinet settles or hinges sag, the doors jam against the frame or show an open space along one or more edges. Overlapping and lip doors cover the cabinet's opening, making minor sags unnoticeable. Lip doors have a ⅜" or ½" rabbet around their perimeters. If the edges of an overlapping door are beveled (30°), they will accept common offset hinges and won't need handles or pulls. You can make a lip door by gluing a ¼" panel onto a ⅜" panel, as shown.

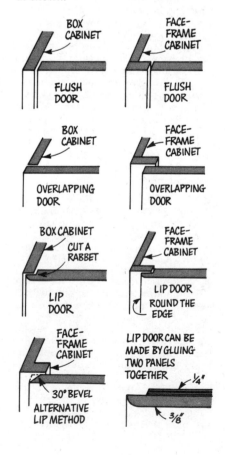

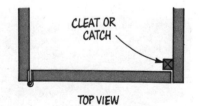

Single flush doors *need stops. Either use a catch (see next page) or fasten a block to the closing side, bottom, or top of the cabinet.*

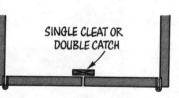

Double flush doors *can be stopped against a cleat fastened to the top or bottom of the cabinet or against a pair of catches (or a double catch).*

Butt hinges come in all shapes and sizes. They can hang both overlapping and flush doors. Unless you use decorative or strap ("T") hinges, only the pin loops of the hinge will show. Decorative and strap hinges—probably the easiest hinges to install—are screwed to the faces of the door and cabinet (they only work on flush doors). Loose-pin hinges allow you to remove the door by pulling out the hinge pins. Continuous ("piano") hinges can be purchased in lengths up to 6' and can then be cut to exact size, using a hacksaw.

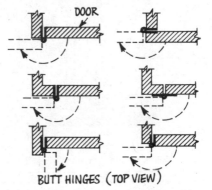

BUTT HINGES (TOP VIEW)

Attach butt hinges to cabinets using any of the methods shown. When attached so only pin loops show, the hinge leaves are mortised (inset) below the wood's surface. You can either mortise the thickness of both leaves in one surface (see page 24 for mortising) or the thickness of one leaf in both surfaces. The mortise reduces the gap between the door and cabinet. To install the door, prop it in the opening with slim wedges, leaving the thickness of a paper match between surfaces. Mark both the door and the case for hinge locations. Outline the mortise with a sharp knife and remove the waste wood with a chisel. Screw the hinges to the door, hold the door in place, and screw the hinges to the cabinet.

Offset hinges are used for hanging lipped or overlapping doors. They are

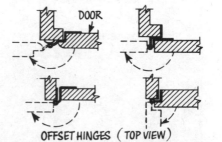

OFFSET HINGES (TOP VIEW)

available in both semi-concealed and surface-mounted styles. Have them on hand before you rabbet doors—the rabbet must match the hinge's offset. To mount them, follow instructions in the package.

Pivot hinges, made for both flush and overlapping doors, come in three main

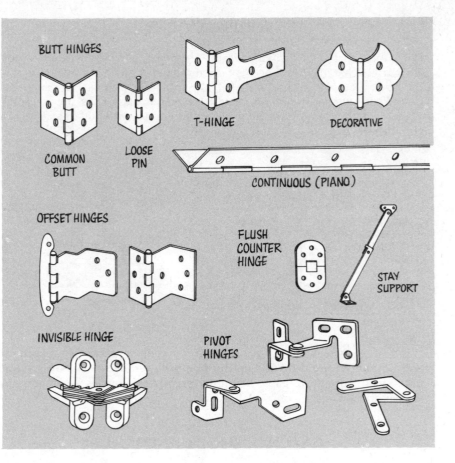

types: side-frame pivot hinges that attach to a door's top and bottom edges, side-frame pivot hinges that attach intermediately along a door's side edge, and top and bottom-mounted "knife" hinges that are quite difficult to install. The three types are shown above. The

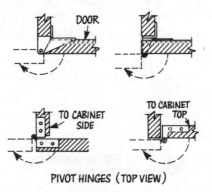

PIVOT HINGES (TOP VIEW)

intermediate type is easiest to install. Pivot hinges are favored in much cabinetry work because only the small pivot shows from the front. Installation instructions are generally included in a package of two.

Invisible hinges don't show from the front. But their installation needs careful attention and they are relatively ex-

INVISIBLE HINGE IS OUT OF SIGHT

TOP SECTION VIEW

pensive. They can be used for both flush and overlapping doors. A template and set of instructions should be included in each package.

Drop-down doors that can be lowered to serve as work surfaces (level with the cabinet's bottom) require hinges that lay flush in the surface. Mortise them into both surfaces; they don't show when the door is closed. A drop-down door also requires a chain or "stay support" to hold the door's weight when it's open.

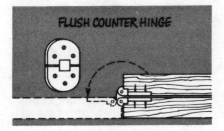

FLUSH COUNTER HINGE

SLIDING DOORS

Flat panels that slide back and forth in grooves, sliding doors are almost always installed in pairs. Since you open the doors by sliding one in front of the other, you can get into only half the cabinet at a time. The panels can be made from almost any thin material including glass or plastic (page 13). The only hardware a sliding door might require is a flush pull or lock, unless you install the doors using track hardware.

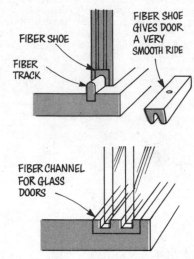

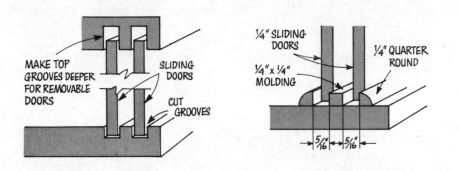

Either grooves or tracks run along the front edge of a cabinet at both top and bottom. When extended up the side walls, grooves lock out dust and hide small side-fitting gaps. Methods for making grooves and tracks are shown at right.

CATCHES, KNOBS, AND PULLS

Other important cabinet door hardware are catches and knobs, or pulls. A few typical styles are shown. When selecting a catch, consider the work it will do. For cabinets subject to constant use, choose solid types not likely to loosen or bend and not dependent on strict alignment (magnetic catches are favorites).

You'll find a wide variety of knobs, drawer pulls, and handles at hardware stores and builders' supply houses; even more styles can be special ordered from catalogs. They come in practically any material you might want: wood, plastic, aluminum, steel, porcelain, and so forth. Match their style to the cabinet. Always add knobs and other hardware that you don't want painted *after* painting the project.

Although small doors can be fitted with light-duty knobs, strong pulls and handles are needed for opening heavy doors and drawers. Place handles above the center of drawer fronts.

THREE KINDS OF CATCHES

DOUBLE ROLLER

FRICTION

MAGNETIC

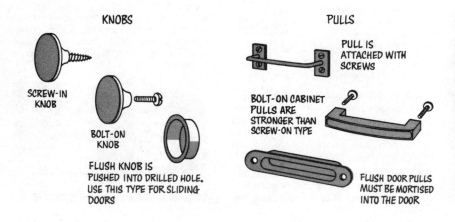

Custom-made handles *lend drawers and doors a touch of elegance. These were cut from small blocks of hardwood.*

Mounting shelves in cabinets

Adding a few shelves to the inside of a cabinet can help you organize its contents and increase the number of things it will hold. The methods given here show how to support shelves from both ends when installing them in

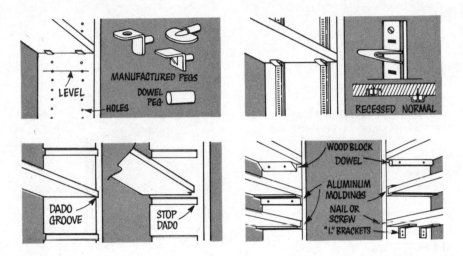

MANUFACTURED PEGS
DOWEL PEG
LEVEL
HOLES
RECESSED   NORMAL

DADO GROOVE
STOP DADO

WOOD BLOCK
DOWEL
ALUMINUM MOLDINGS
NAIL OR SCREW
"L" BRACKETS

Far left. *Drilled holes and pegs are strong, adjustable, and usually unnoticeable. Be sure to keep holes level.*

Near left. *Brackets and clips make shelves highly adjustable. Mount the brackets flush or recess them.*

Far left. *Dado grooves are cut for permanent or adjustable shelves. The stop dado can't be seen from the front.*

Near left. *Shelf holders can be made from practically any type of block, bar, or bracket. Shown are several ideas.*

cabinets or closets. If the shelves can't stretch a certain span without bowing, add support across their back edges. (See more about making shelves on page 37.)

Legs, casters, & tension devices

Unless a cabinet is hung from a wall or ceiling (page 50), it may need to be raised off the floor; this will make its contents more reachable, make it easy to clean under, and keep you from kicking the base when you step close to it. It can be raised by several kinds of supports. Some of these—typical bases, legs, feet, and casters—are shown on this page.

Below a cabinet's base or legs, a threaded tension device can level the cabinet by raising or lowering a corner. On a backless, floor-to-ceiling, freestanding unit, these devices can wedge the unit against the ceiling, keeping it rigid without nails, screws, or other fasteners (to see these devices in action, turn to the projects on page 62 or 70).

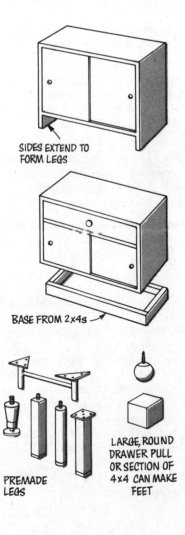

SIDES EXTEND TO FORM LEGS

BASE FROM 2x4s

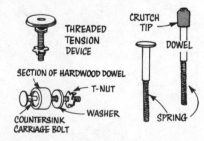

THREADED TENSION DEVICE
CRUTCH TIP
DOWEL
SECTION OF HARDWOOD DOWEL
T-NUT
COUNTERSINK CARRIAGE BOLT
WASHER
SPRING

HEAVY-DUTY CASTER
BALL-TYPE CASTER

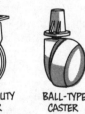

PREMADE LEGS

LARGE, ROUND DRAWER PULL OR SECTION OF 4x4 CAN MAKE FEET

Tension devices *wedge a shelving unit between ceiling and floor. Threaded type might be called "appliance levelers."*

Casters *mobilize shelving units and cabinets. Some types are made for rolling on carpets, others for hard flooring.*

How to make & install drawers

Drawers can really expand a cabinet's storage capacity. When closed, drawer contents are protected and out of view; when open, everything inside is easily accessible.

Although you can buy premade drawers in standard sizes from home-improvement centers and lumberyards and design the cabinets to fit them, making your own drawers is a bit more challenging and much cheaper. This section will tell you how it is done.

DRAWER SELECTION

Have a clear idea of the kind of drawer you want to make well before you begin construction. For familiarization, read through all the following information about drawers:

Appearance. Drawer fronts are cut to fit cabinets the same way doors are. They can completely overlap the edges of a cabinet, partially lip the cabinet, sit flush with the face of the cabinet, or inset. Consider the appearance you wish the cabinet to have before choosing the method of cutting and joining.

Cabinet type. Drawers fit box cabinets and face-frame cabinets differently. Before making a drawer, consider the type of cabinet it will go into and the system of guides that will be used to steer it. The cabinet and guide method will often affect the width of the drawer, its height, and its depth. Turn the page for information on cabinet types and guiding methods.

Construction methods. On the facing page, you can see how drawers are put together. Choose a design that is strong, won't eventually fall apart, and will work within the limits of your skills and tools.

CHOOSING DRAWER MATERIALS

One of the main objects in drawer construction is to make the drawer strong enough to hold its contents but as lightweight as possible. Therefore, the size and amount of materials you use is critical. Solid pine and fir are excellent for drawer fronts, sides, and backs, particularly when you'll be cutting dadoes and rabbets. But watch out for one thing: large pieces (like 1 by 10s or 1 by 12s) may tend to warp. Unless you can find very straight, kiln-dried wood, choose plywood for deep drawers. A good thickness for a drawer front is ¾". Making the sides and back from ½" or ⅝" material will help keep the weight down, but if you plan to dado grooves into the sides for runners, pick ¾" stock. Choose a bottom material that is strong enough to hold the drawer's contents without bowing—¼" hardboard is a favorite because it's smooth, stiff, and doesn't warp.

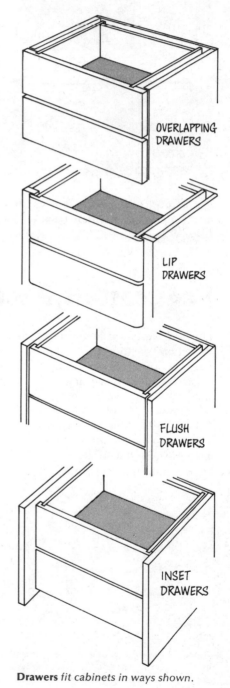

OVERLAPPING DRAWERS

LIP DRAWERS

FLUSH DRAWERS

INSET DRAWERS

Drawers *fit cabinets in ways shown.*

CONSTRUCTION

Although some drawer construction methods call for a cabinetmaker's skill, anyone can make at least one of the types shown here with a minimum of tools and woodworking skill. Regardless of how you build it, every drawer will normally require the same number of cuts (and those made with power tools will need the same number of rabbet grooves and dadoes). Your work time can be shortened by standardizing procedures; repeat the same grooves and cuts for several drawers. For example, for drawers of the same size, cut the bottoms all at once. Do the same for sides, fronts, and backs. If you dado the bottom in place, cut the dadoes in fronts and sides all at the same time. (A table saw or radial-arm saw is an excellent tool for repeating identical cuts.)

Be sure to cut all pieces exactly and remember to allow 3/32" between the drawer and the frame, leaving the drawer room to slide. Notice that you can eliminate the need for a drawer stop for flush or recessed drawers by insetting the back and bottom about ½" into the sides and later trimming the sides to stop the drawer against the back at the proper place.

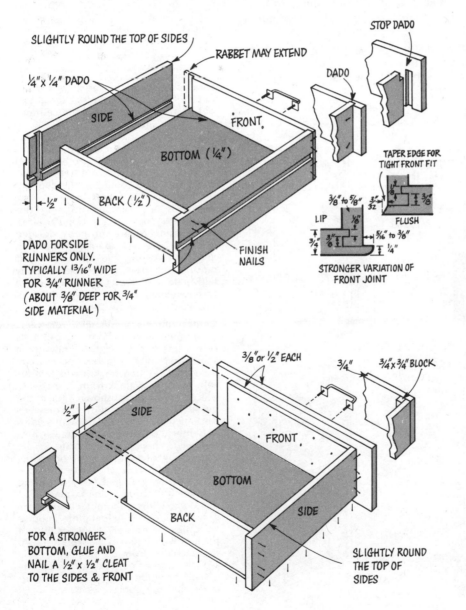

Using power tools. The dadoes or rabbets required for making this drawer are the reasons you need a power tool. (For information on cutting dadoes and rabbets, see page 26.)

Begin by cutting and grooving all the pieces. Be sure to cut the bottom square at all four corners. Assemble the pieces without glue to check for proper fit; then use glue in all joints for final assembly. First place the drawer front face down on a padded surface and fit the bottom into place. Then fit the side to the front. If possible, drive four nails in dovetail fashion as shown, to hold the pieces together until the glue sets. Otherwise, use clamps when the drawer is assembled (see pages 28 and 29). Next, fit the back between the sides, inset about ½", and nail it through the sides. Turn the drawer upside down and drive several nails through the bottom into the back. Slightly round the top edges of the sides.

Without power tools. If you don't have the tools necessary for cutting dadoes, this drawer is the one for you. Cut the pieces to size; then check them for proper fit before gluing them together. The bottom must be square at all four corners.

To form the drawer front, brad and glue a ⅜" or ½" panel to another ⅜" or ½" panel, as shown. Then glue and nail the sides to the inner panel. Or to help keep the drawer's weight down, you can glue and screw a ¾" by ¾" block to each side; then glue and screw through each block to the front. Turn the unit on its side after fitting the back in place and glue and nail it to each side. If the drawer won't be holding heavy items, glue and nail the bottom flush to the lower edge of each side, the back, and the inside front panel. Otherwise, nail a ¼" by ¼" strip around the lower inside perimeter of the sides and front to hold the bottom in place.

(Continued on next page)

INSTALLING DRAWER GUIDES

Unless a drawer is small enough to slide freely in a box-like enclosure, it must be steered in and out so it won't bind. Two main types of guides perform this job: side guides and center guides. Side guides work for most drawers, holding the weight from each side while steering the drawer. Center guides must be mounted on face frames, for they only guide the drawer (the weight must be supported along a side rail or shelf). Because they require more framing, waste the space between drawers, and are more difficult to install, center guides are recommended only for very wide drawers.

Most guides are a sort of runner-and-groove arrangement. The runner is usually a narrow piece of hardwood. The groove can be a channeled piece of stock, a space between two runners, or a groove dadoed into the drawer or cabinet. Manufactured guides cost most than the homemade variety, but are well worth the money. These roller-and-track systems can give even the heaviest of drawers a smooth ride, allowing them to be fully extended and installed without making special cuts. Manufactured center guides can carry drawers in a face-frame cabinet without additional rails or framing for holding the drawer's weight. Instructions for installation of manufactured guides are offered on the packages.

To make wooden guides operate smoothly, first coat them with sealer; then either paint them with shellac and steel-wool them until smooth, wax them, or lubricate them with a spray that's made for the purpose.

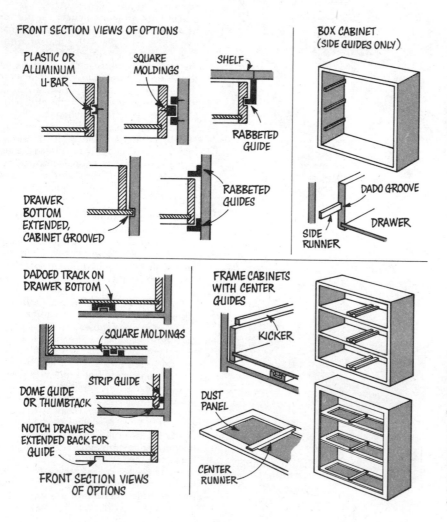

FRONT SECTION VIEWS OF OPTIONS

PLASTIC OR ALUMINUM U-BAR

SQUARE MOLDINGS

SHELF

RABBETED GUIDE

DRAWER BOTTOM EXTENDED, CABINET GROOVED

RABBETED GUIDES

BOX CABINET (SIDE GUIDES ONLY)

DADO GROOVE

DRAWER

SIDE RUNNER

DADOED TRACK ON DRAWER BOTTOM

SQUARE MOLDINGS

STRIP GUIDE

DOME GUIDE OR THUMBTACK

NOTCH DRAWER'S EXTENDED BACK FOR GUIDE

FRONT SECTION VIEWS OF OPTIONS

FRAME CABINETS WITH CENTER GUIDES

KICKER

DUST PANEL

CENTER RUNNER

Side guides carry drawers in either box or face-frame cabinets (block the guides out to meet the drawer in a face-frame cabinet). A side guide is usually a hardwood runner attached to the cabinet that fits in a groove in the drawer's side, as shown. The drawer's groove should be about 1/16" wider and deeper than the runner (and about half the depth of the drawer's side material). Be sure the runner is large enough to hold the weight (½" by ¾" is a popular size). When runners are properly located (measure and tack them into position and then try out the fit), mark their placement and fasten them permanently with glue and screws or nails (be sure to countersink fasteners). Variations of side guides are shown here.

Center runners guide wide drawers. Each runner is attached to the cabinet's face frame and back; extra rails (or a shelf) support the drawer. You can buy a dadoed wooden track, dado it yourself, or make a track from two square pieces of stock as shown. Make the guide thin enough to allow the drawer's bottom to set ½" up from the sides.

Center the guide on the drawer bottom first; then place its mate in the cabinet by measuring from one side. Tack it temporarily, check its workability, and then glue and screw or nail it permanently (countersink fasteners).

A dome glide or thumbtack under the drawer's sides will help it glide smoothly. Unless a drawer is locked into a track, it will require a "kicker" to keep the back end from popping up as you pull the drawer out. The kicker can be a shelf or guide above the drawer, or a wooden bar above the drawer.

Easy drawer alternatives

If, after looking through the drawer construction methods, you've decided to sidestep making drawers, here are some inexpensive drawer alternatives, such as molded plastic containers, baking pans, and cardboard boxes. (Premade drawers can also be purchased at home-improvement centers or from cabinetmakers.)

Molded plastic containers can organize clothing, sewing gear, craft materials, or a variety of objects. Durable and lightweight, they are available at department stores in many styles and colors. Those shown are installed in a bedroom closet behind sliding doors. They have a lip that rides in a groove made from wooden runners, as shown. Design: Ernest J. Kump Associates.

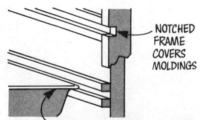

NOTCHED FRAME COVERS MOLDINGS

LIP OF PLASTIC BIN RIDES IN A TRACK MADE OF TWO SQUARE MOLDINGS

Tin baking pans with porcelain pulls become small drawers in this sewing storage cabinet built from rough-cut redwood fencing. To build the unit, first join horizontal shelves in the middle with corrugated fasteners. Then notch horizontal and vertical pieces so they join as shown in the diagram. Cut notches 3" deep and wide enough to prevent the wood from splitting when slipped together. Finally, construct a simple frame around the grid with redwood fencing, fastening with glue and 3-penny nails. Attach to wall studs (page 50) using L-brackets. Design: Rick Morrall.

CORRUGATED FASTENERS

3" NOTCHES

½" x 6" REDWOOD FENCING

Twenty-one cardboard boxes form drawers in this simple, knock-down storage unit that's made from two sheets of ¼" tempered hardboard and cotton rope.

Although the uniform, plain brown boxes were purchased from a carton factory, you could collect boxes from stores and alter the unit's design to fit them. If you wish, paint or cover them with decorative paper.

A power saw is very useful for cutting hardboard. If you don't have one, consider having the major cuts made at the lumberyard. For horizontal shelves, cut a 4' by 8' sheet of tempered hardboard lengthwise into four pieces 11⅞" wide and then notch them as shown. From a second sheet of hardboard, cut eight vertical pieces 44" long and 11⅞" wide and notch them as shown. Round corners of all pieces and sand edges smooth.

Assemble the unit by pushing the pieces together. Then lay it front down and square the corners. Cotton rope pushed through eight ¼" holes in the back and crosstied as shown provides the bracing needed to keep the unit square. Design: Gary Fitschen.

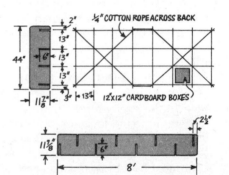

¼" COTTON ROPE ACROSS BACK

2"
13"
44"
6"
13"
13"
11⅞"
3" 13¾"
12"x12" CARDBOARD BOXES

2½"
11⅞"
6"
8'

Fastening to walls & ceilings

Most house walls and ceilings are not solid. They generally consist of such sheet materials as gypsum wallboard or plaster and lath applied over a framework of wall studs and ceiling joists. Studs and joists can clench nails and screws firmly, but the wall-covering materials alone don't have the necessary resiliency. Therefore, when fastening between studs or joists, you'll have to either provide the necessary framing by bridging the gaps with cross members or, for hanging relatively light shelving and other lightweight fastening jobs, use special hollow-wall fasteners.

Masonry walls are another story. Concrete, brick, tile, and other masonry surfaces generally require an anchoring sleeve that, once pushed into a hole, receives a screw or bolt, expanding the sleeve to a tight fit. (Concrete nails, also useful under some circumstances, are discussed on page 30.)

FINDING HIDDEN STUDS & JOISTS

To gain the strength provided by such common fasteners as nails, you have to determine the location of wall studs or ceiling joists. Unless a room has unfinished walls or an open-beam ceiling, finding those support members can be a problem. Here's how to do it.

In most houses, wall studs and ceiling joists are spaced regularly. Often you can locate studs by measuring from a corner. At the house's four major corners, measure in 14½" to find the center of the first stud; the rest should fall every 16" (sometimes 20" or 24"). At other minor corners, the first stud is probably 16" in. Ceiling joists run parallel to two walls, spaced evenly and in line with the studs of the other two walls.

Sometimes you can see the nails that hold wall-paneling materials to studs, but nails in gypsum wallboard are usually hidden. An inexpensive "stud finder" will help you locate them. This handy little tool has a magnetized needle that fluctuates when passed over a nail. If the wall paneling was applied with adhesive rather than nails, you'll have to try another method. Check for nails holding paneling or siding to the other side of the wall; measure their location from a corner or a doorway and transfer the measurements to the proper side of the wall.

Knocking firmly on the wall with the heel of your clenched fist will sometimes enable you to locate studs. Rap sharply in the area where you think a stud should be. A solid sound means a stud is beneath; a hollow sound tells you to keep knocking.

If all else fails, make exploratory holes, using a small drill or nail. Either drill a hair's breadth above the base molding and fill the holes later or take up the molding and drill where the hole will be covered. If the bit reaches solid wood, you have either found a stud or penetrated into the "sole plate"

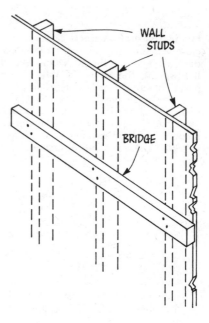

Hang heavy bookshelves *and cabinets on walls either by fastening directly to wall studs or by bridging studs as shown and then fastening to the bridge.*

(a flat 2 by 4 to which the lower ends of stud are nailed). After you are sure you've found a stud, try locating the rest by measuring and knocking.

To locate joists, measure (keeping in mind the fact that joists only run in one direction), use a stud finder, try knocking, or probe with a small nail. On the top floor of a house, you may be able to crawl into the attic and see their placement and even add support blocking between joists. If the room has a suspended ceiling, just push one of the panels up to look for strong support.

HOLLOW-WALL FASTENERS

When fastening directly to studs or joists is out of the question, select a fastener that will umbrella out or expand once pushed into the wall or ceiling. Three types of hollow-wall fasteners are shown.

Spreading anchors are applied in two ways: one is carefully driven into the wall; the other is pushed into a hole. Once inserted, they both work in the same way—turn the screw clockwise until fairly tight (permanently anchoring the sleeve), remove the screw, push it through a hole in the cabinet or fixture you're hanging, and screw it snugly back into the sleeve. If abandoned, the sleeve must be set slightly below the wall's surface and the hole then filled.

Toggle bolts require drilling a hole large enough to push the wings through, so they're meant for permanently fastening fixtures that will hide the holes. Insert the screw through the cabinet or fixture first, spin the wings part way on, squeeze them together, and push them through the wall's hole. Once inside the wall, the wings spring open. Then tighten the bolt (don't overtighten). If for some reason you need to remove the bolt, the wings will fall inside the wall. (A gravity-action toggle bolt is basically the same, but when pushed through a wall's hole, the sleeve drops into position.)

Neoprene anchors, though not as strong as the other two fasteners, are versatile enough to use in both hollow walls and masonry walls. They require a relatively small hole and are removable. Drill a hole (slightly deeper than the sleeve's length in masonry), insert the sleeve, position the cabinet or fixture, push the screw through it into the sleeve, and tighten while holding the fixture against the sleeve to keep it from turning.

MASONRY FASTENERS

Fiber, neoprene, vinyl, and lead anchors receive screws and bolts in masonry. (Lead anchors are the strongest.) Another type of masonry fastener is the stud anchor. This doesn't receive a screw or bolt—instead, it leaves a threaded shaft protruding from the wall, to which you add a nut.

When using a masonry fastener, drill a hole the same diameter as the anchor and slightly deeper than its length. A carbide bit in a ½" electric drill is best; drilling with a hammer and star drill takes considerably more patience. If you use a star drill, mark the exact center of the hole and hold the drill firmly while making the first five or six hammer taps. Once the hole begins to form, loosen your grip and let the drill tip dance a little as you strike. Use hundreds of light taps rather than dozens of crushing blows. Always wear eye protection when drilling masonry.

Once the hole is drilled, push in the anchor shield and insert the screw or bolt through the cabinet or fixture, screwing it into the anchor. If an anchor eventually works loose, discard it and use another.

Spreading stud anchors are very simple to install. Push the entire device through a hole in the cabinet or fixture and then into a hole in the masonry. As you tighten down the nut, the anchor expands in the wall.

SPREADING ANCHOR

1. INSERT ANCHOR & BOLT IN HOLE

2. TIGHTEN BOLT TO SPREAD SLEEVE

3. REMOVE BOLT, PUSH THROUGH FIXTURE, AND TIGHTEN IT

TOGGLE BOLT

1. PASS BOLT THROUGH FIXTURE

2. PUSH THROUGH HOLE IN WALL

3. WINGS SPRING OPEN. TIGHTEN BOLT

NEOPRENE ANCHOR

1. DRILL HOLE. INSERT ANCHOR

2. PUSH BOLT THROUGH FIXTURE. INSERT IN SLEEVE & TIGHTEN, HOLDING FIXTURE AGAINST SLEEVE

CARBIDE BIT FOR POWER DRILL

STAR DRILL

HEAVY DUTY LEAD ANCHOR

STUD ANCHOR

Finishing techniques

When you complete the construction of a project, it's usually a good idea to add a finish to the wood. Finishes can protect wood from becoming easily dented, stained, or soiled, and they can enhance the appearance of most woods.

CHOOSING A FINISH

The multitude of available finishing products is confusing, if not bewildering. Although this short section can't attempt to explain all there is to know about various finishes (Sunset's companion book, *Furniture Finishing & Refinishing* does that), it can familiarize you with the most common types. Armed with this basic understanding, you can select particular finishes with help from your local paint dealer.

The chart on the facing page divides common finishes into three groups: clear finishes, stains, and enamels. The earlier you decide which group you'll use, the better. If possible, decide before buying materials. That way, you can buy the wood or material that will best suit the appearance you want. Low-grade woods and sheet materials, such as plywood, may be adequate for a project being painted — the enamel will cover unsightly qualities. Light-colored, medium-grade woods stain well (the more opaque the stain, the lower the wood's quality may be). The beauty of high-grade, fine woods can be captured by natural finishes; they often make the wood look wet, enhancing its grain and color.

Beyond appearance, consider some of the following traits before selecting a finish.

Texture. Many finishes — polyurethane, varnish, and enamels, to name a few — coat the wood, making it feel very smooth but covering its natural texture. Finishes that soak in—Danish oil, penetrating resin, and most stains, for example—leave the natural feel of the wood. Also consider the sheen of the finish: gloss finishes have high reflectance; satin finishes have very low reflectance.

Durability. Projects subject to continual use require hard, abuse-tolerant finishes. Gloss enamels (particularly alkyd-based) are extremely durable paints. Polyurethane and varnish can add durability to either stained or natural wood.

Application. Although most of today's finishing products are easy to apply,

(Continued on page 54)

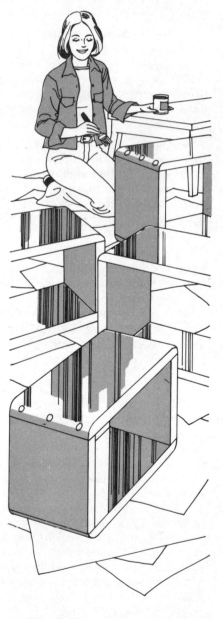

Apply a finish *carefully; it will be the most visible part of your workmanship. When choosing one, consider its transparency, shade or color, texture, durability, and ease of application.*

CHARACTERISTICS OF COMMON FINISHES

CLEAR FINISHES	Advantages	Disadvantages	General Traits
SHELLAC	Doesn't mar easily. Very fast drying.	Soluble in alcohol, ammonia, detergent. Not moisture-proof.	Coats surface. Tends to slightly darken light-toned woods.
VARNISH	Alcohol, chemical, heat, impact, water resistant.	Careful sanding required between coats. Slow drying.	Coats surface. Provides a rough, slightly amber-tinted finish.
POLYURETHANE	Easy to apply. Fast drying. Tough, resilient, very smooth.	Cleans up with mineral spirits.	Coats surface. Enhances wood grain with slight darkening effect.
LACQUER	Primes, seals, finishes in one step. Abrasion resistant. Very fast drying.	Can be used only over bare wood or lacquer. Thins, cleans up with lacquer thinner.	Coats surface. High lustre. Available both in spray can and brush-on.
PENETRATING RESIN FINISH	Easy to apply with rag. Very durable.	Timing of application is critical. Cleans up with mineral spirits.	Soaks into wood rather than coating the surface.
DANISH OIL	Easy to apply with rag. Helps wood repel moisture.	Requires several coats for stain resistance. Won't protect wood from marring.	Soaks into wood rather than coating surface.

STAINS			
ALCOHOL STAIN	Applied with rag. Very short drying time (although this can be a problem).	Practice needed for application. Fairly expensive. Thins, cleans up with alcohol.	Very transparent, does not camouflage wood. Cool in tone (with slight greenish tint).
PENETRATING OIL STAIN	Easy to apply with rag. Can be bleached out of wood if results undesirable.	Long drying time. Cleans up with mineral spirits.	Soaks into wood rather than coating it.
PIGMENTED WIPING STAIN	Easy to apply with rag. Can be given additional coats.	Too dark for many uses. Timing of application is critical. Cleans up with mineral spirits.	Very opaque — makes one wood species look like another in color.
WATER STAIN	Thins, cleans up with water.	Very slow drying. Raises wood grain slightly. Difficult to apply without practice.	Transparent stain (lets wood grain show). Wide variety of shades.

ENAMELS			
OIL-BASED ENAMEL	High durability. Washable. Good adhesion, covers well.	Slow drying. Requires enamel undercoat. Mineral spirits required for clean up, thinning.	Totally hides wood. Available in gloss and semi-gloss and in all colors.
LATEX ENAMEL	Good leveling properties. Dries quickly. Thins, cleans up with water.	Doesn't hold up under constant wear. Coverage less than that of oil-based enamel.	Totally hides wood. Available in semi-gloss in all colors.

some are not. Read the directions on the container before buying a finish to see the number of steps and amount of time necessary for application.

PREPARING THE WOOD

Since a finish can be no better than the surface to which it's applied, careful preparation is important for successful finishing. Surfaces should be smooth and free of scratches, cracks, holes, and other imperfections. After you fill any cracks or holes, sand the surface conscientiously to eliminate scratches and minor irregularities.

Filling imperfections

The proper methods and materials for filling defects in wood depend upon the finish you intend to give the project. A clear finish requires carefully filling the wood with a patching product that won't show through. Stains, especially the transparent ones, can magnify the presence of some patching products. You can use practically any filler on a surface that is to be covered with enamel.

For a natural finish. Fill blemishes with wood dough or stick shellac (a specialty product used by furniture makers). Both products come in colors that match most woods. You spread wood dough with a putty knife; stick shellac is melted into the hole or crack. When patching large holes, fill the hole, let the patching compound dry, sand the surface on and around the patch, and repeat the process. Always build up the compound slightly above the surface and then sand off the excess.

Before finishing a knotty wood, seal the knots with shellac — this will prevent sap from seeping through. Do this whether you're applying a natural finish, staining, or painting.

When staining. Because none of the patching compounds dry at the same porosity as woods, they tend to absorb stain differently. For this reason, fillers often show up under a stain. Choose a wood dough that is closest to the color the wood will be *after* it is stained (you may want to try out the stain on a scrap piece of the wood first). Dark stains and opaque stains usually camouflage fillers best (dark stains also alter the identity of a wood most convincingly).

When painting. Practically any filler works for surfaces being enameled. Spackling compound is a good choice; it is inexpensive, easy to use, penetrates well, and is easy to clean up. You can also try a thick mixture of fine sawdust and white glue for filling cracks. (Although a glue-and-sawdust mixture takes on the appearance of the wood, this mixture does not make a good filler for surfaces to be stained; the glue-covered area will not accept the pigments of the stain.)

Sanding

Crucial for a successful finish, sanding requires a good eye, patience, and a bit of elbow grease. Power sanders can greatly ease the tedium of sanding — a few of the common types are shown. (Also see a disc-sanding attachment for electric drills on page 23.)

Whether you do it by power or hand, divide sanding into three steps: rough, preparatory (after you've filled defects), and finish. First, rough sand with 80-grit sandpaper. Then do preparatory sanding with 120-grit paper to further smooth the wood, especially where fillers have been used. Finish sand with 180-grit (or finer) paper. The finest finishes are usually those given a final sanding by hand. After sanding, vacuum the surface to remove any dust or wipe it with a rag dampened with mineral spirits. When you're sure it's clear of dust, apply the finish.

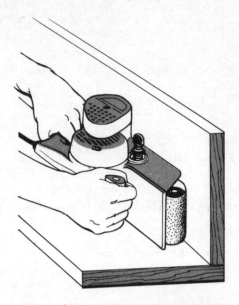

Belt sander *provides the fastest sanding. It must be used in line with grain.*

Orbital sander *removes wood fast and is easy to hold with one hand. Don't use an orbital sander for final sanding.*

In-line sander *is best for final sanding. Be sure base moves in grain's direction.*

APPLICATION TIPS

Although the many different types of finishes are applied differently, most have a few common traits. Here are some tips for applying finishes with brushes:

Choose the right brush for the finish you're applying. Natural-bristle brushes, made from hog's hair, are traditional favorites for applying oil-base enamels, varnish, lacquer, alkyd enamels, polyurethane, and all but the water-based finishes. Though hog bristles are not nearly as long-lasting as nylon, most painters feel they have superior brushing qualities. The better ones hold more paint and have more intricately "flagged" bristles (see photo) than synthetic brushes. On the other hand, synthetic brushes, usually nylon, are less expensive, wear exceptionally well, and work better for water-based finishes because they absorb less water than natural brushes. Although they can apply most kinds of finishes, don't use them for lacquer or shellac (the solvents in these finishes tend to soften nylon).

Choose a brush that is full. Bounce the bristles against the back of your hand to check them for fullness and springiness. Remember, too, that the longer the bristles your brush has, the more paint it will hold. Pick a convenient width for the job you have in mind.

Hold the brush comfortably. Most people prefer holding a brush near the base of its handle. Press lightly downward with your fingertips, slightly flexing the bristles toward the tip at the beginning of each stroke.

Dip the brush about one-third of the bristles' length into the finish. Then, when the brush is full, wipe the tip lightly against the inside lip of the container to catch drips. (Keep a rag dampened with solvent nearby for cleaning up drips and spatters.)

Brush slowly. Rapidly applying finishes causes them to skip and collect air bubbles. Slow brushing forces the finish into tiny depressions in the surface, insuring better coverage.

Keep coverage consistent. Apply the paint or finish rather liberally at first. Then brush it out thoroughly with slow, even strokes. Minimize brush marks by keeping your brush from getting too dry. If the wood has open pores or checks, cross brush the finish into the wood: first, brush the finish on in one direction (normally across the grain); then brush across it, this time with the grain, to level it. This forces the finish down into the wood's irregularities.

Examine bristle ends to see if most are "flagged" (naturally or artificially divided). This is good flagged nylon.

Check springiness by pressing brush against hand. Good bristles spread evenly, feel soft and silky, are clean and straight.

HOW TO FINISH DOUGLAS-FIR PLYWOOD

Douglas-fir plywood, one of the most commonly used building materials, looks natural when given a clear finish, looks great when painted properly, but requires special attention when stained. Why? Because the surface veneers of fir plywood are quite grainy — made up of swirls of both hard and soft wood fibers. These fibers absorb stains unevenly: the soft fibers absorb the majority of a stain, whereas the hard fibers practically repel it. The plywood's resulting appearance is very grainy. It usually looks like a piece of plywood that someone tried, but failed, to make look like something else.

Before staining, equalize the absorption rate between the hard and soft wood fibers by applying two liberal coats of "orange" shellac (it is actually clear), mixing it with equal parts denatured alcohol first. When this coating dries, sand the plywood's surface thoroughly to remove the shellac from the hard fibers while leaving the absorbed portion as a sealer in the soft fibers. This way, the stain isn't absorbed so readily by the soft fibers. Then apply the stain. When it dries, spray it with a can of clear lacquer to stabilize the color. If you wish, you can then build up a final finish with additional coats of varnish or polyurethane.

The same grain characteristics can be a problem if you want to give plywood a very smooth coat of enamel. You can overcome this by first applying a coat of penetrating sealer to stabilize absorption. Sand between successive coats of enamel.

For a very fine painted surface, you might prefer to use resin-overlaid plywood (page 11). Grain raise and checking don't show with this type because a resin-impregnated paper covers the wood.

See more about plywood — veneer types, grading, sizing, and so forth— on page 10. Also find methods of treating plywood edges on that page.

Step-by-step projects
Forty-two designs...simple but attractive

Wall systems, stackable modules, basic shelving, wall-hung storage boards, bars and kitchen cabinets — this section offers a potpourri of easy-to-make projects. Thumb through the pages to find one that suits you (or use the directory at right). Once you do, you'll be on the road to owning a project like it — making it is simply a matter of following directions. Read what the project is all about to determine the tools and materials you'll need to have on hand; then just work according to the procedures. Before you know it, you'll be using the completed unit and starting to make another.

Plastic pipe provides *the support for this shelving system (see page 74).*

PROJECTS DIRECTORY

Modular cabinets *(see page 86) were designed with an awareness of low cost, easy construction, and stylish appearance. Use them for storage in any part of the house.*

Stackable cubes (see page 64), made from heavy lumber, don't require backs. Make them to fit your stereo equipment, books, plants, or other collectibles; then just stack them up.

Floor-to-ceiling wall system (see page 70) holds shelves, cabinets, a desk — even a seat. It is totally adjustable and, when you want to move it, can be disassembled easily.

Versatile kitchen cabinets (see page 92) are built in separate units for kitchen.

Ten ideas for quick & easy shelving

1 Chain-hung shelving. For medium to lightweight loads, shelving fastened to chains is easy to make and inexpensive. Four hooks screwed 1½″ into ceiling joists hold four lengths of chain; shelves are fastened intermediately along the chains using hanger bolts (page 35), washers and nuts as shown. The shelves can be adjusted up or down along the chain links. Because the unit has very little lateral stability, you should locate it where it won't be bumped by passersby. Anchor the bottom ends of chains by fastening them to the floor or wall or place heavy items on the bottom shelf. For information on finding ceiling joists, see page 50.

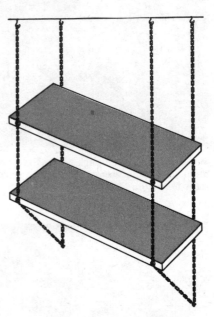

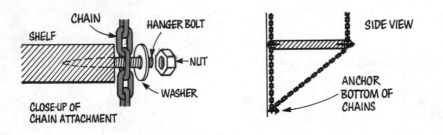

2 Suspended shelves. One efficient way to add storage shelves where ceiling joists are exposed — in attics, basements, or garages — is to hang them as shown. Although most ceiling joists easily can hold the added weight, fasten shelving that will bear heavy loads to several joists, near the walls or posts that hold the joists.

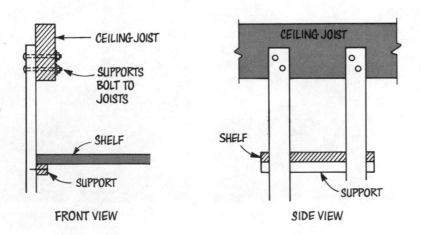

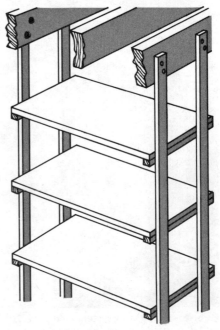

3 Blocks and boards. During the last few years, one of the most popular make-it-fast shelving designs (especially for the mobile student population) has been blocks and boards. Making this kind of shelving is easy and requires no tools. You buy shelving boards and precast concrete or cinder blocks at the lumberyard and stack them alternately. Either leave the pieces natural or paint them. One note about their mobility: if you plan to move often, keep in mind the fact that concrete blocks are not the lightest of shelving supports (something like the lightweight plastic-pipe shelving on page 74 is easier to move).

A wide range of both decorative and not-so-decorative concrete and cinder blocks are available; if you can't decide which to choose, mix them (but check to be sure all pairs are the same size). Or, instead of concrete blocks, try using bricks, large wooden blocks, or rectangular tile drain pipes.

4 Shelves and nylon webbing. Novel in that it isn't made entirely from wood, this unit has shelves that get their primary support from straps of woven nylon. You can buy the nylon webbing in rolls, packaged for reweaving lawn furniture, at practically any hardware store. The supports could also be made from canvas or leather. (Canvas may tend to stretch and must be seamed along its edges so it won't fray; leather is a better substitute.)

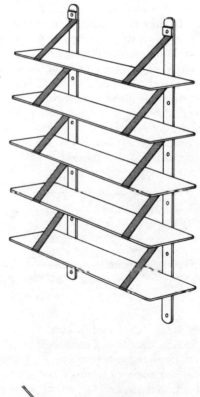

Assemble the unit before hanging it on the wall. Screw hanger bolts in the back edges of the shelves; then drill and countersink holes for them in the uprights. Cut ten lengths of the webbing about 20" long. Beginning with the top shelf, fasten the first two webbing straps in place under the blocks and push the shelf's hanger bolts through the second pair of straps and into the upright's holes. Tighten nuts on the hanger bolts. Pull the top straps tightly around the front edge of the top shelf and, holding the shelf at 90° to the supports, lag screw each strap to the shelf's underside as shown. Trim off the excess webbing. Repeat these assembly procedures for the remaining shelves. Design: Donald Wm. MacDonald, AIA.

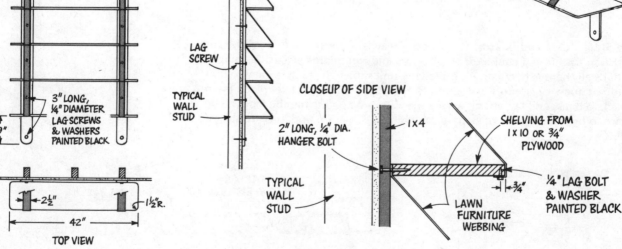

FRONT VIEW

WOOD BLOCK FROM 1x4

1¾"
2½"
12"
1x4
3" LONG, ¼" DIAMETER LAG SCREWS & WASHERS PAINTED BLACK
9"

2½"
1½" R.
42"

TOP VIEW

SIDE VIEW

LAG SCREW

TYPICAL WALL STUD

CLOSEUP OF SIDE VIEW

2" LONG, ¼" DIA. HANGER BOLT

1x4

SHELVING FROM 1 x 10 OR ¾" PLYWOOD

TYPICAL WALL STUD

¾"

LAWN FURNITURE WEBBING

¼" LAG BOLT & WASHER PAINTED BLACK

5 **Wooden wall standards and brackets.** You don't have to buy metal wall standards and brackets to hang adjustable shelves on a wall. Consider making your own from wood as shown. As you can see, the principle can even be expanded to hang cabinets. The wall standards are 1 by 2s with holes drilled through the edges every 2". Attach the standards to wall studs (page 50) using three or four 2½" lag bolts for each (be sure holes in the two standards will be matching levels so shelves won't tilt). The shelves have permanent wooden sides (¼" hardboard works well) that work as both supporting brackets and bookends. The sides have holes drilled 4" apart that match the holes through the standards. Just push bolts or dowels through to support shelves at the proper height.

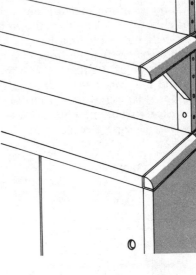

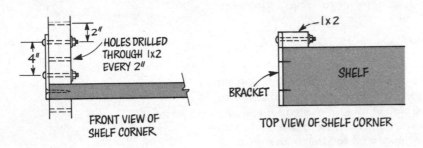

FRONT VIEW OF SHELF CORNER

TOP VIEW OF SHELF CORNER

6 **Aluminum molding and wooden wall standards.** Aluminum molding screwed to shelf ends and cabinet corners can support shelves and cabinets and enhance their appearance. This method works especially well where you want to make fine cabinets and shelves from high-grade, hardwood-veneered plywood but don't want the plywood edges to show (cover the front edges using solid wood or veneer tape). Cut the ¾" by ¾" angle molding as shown, drill a ¼" hole in the protruding flange, screw the molding in place (see sketch), add a piece of solid wood with glue, and then round the wood's corner, sanding wood and aluminum together. Make the standard as described in the above project (number 5).

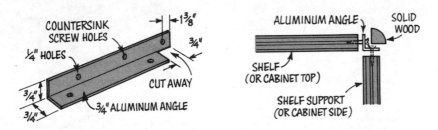

7 **Stepladders and boards.** What easier way is there to make bookshelves than to set up a couple of stepladders and run boards across the rungs? That's all there is to making the shelving unit shown. Just buy a pair of stepladders (new or used), finish them to the appearance you like, place them back to back, and lay boards across the rungs. When buying the ladders, be sure to buy two that have steps at matching heights. Two options are shown below.

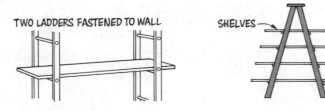

TWO LADDERS FASTENED TO WALL

SHELVES

USE SINGLE STEP LADDER BY FASTENING CLEATS ON BACK SIDE

8 Permanent wall shelving. Here is a shelving method that is excellent for lots of storage in a basement or garage; a more decorative version could work well in any room. To make it, first run 1 by 2 cleats horizontally along the wall at the proper heights for shelves. Screw them to studs (see page 50) with 3" lag screws. The cleats should be the same length as the shelves. Slightly round the front corners of shelves and nail their back edges to the cleats. Nail 1 by 3s or 1 by 4s vertically, extending from floor to ceiling, to the front edge of each shelf for support. The more vertical supports you use, the stronger the shelves will be.

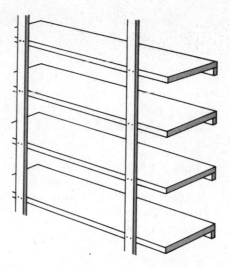

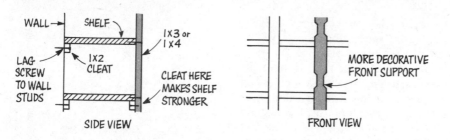

9 Double-sided shelf. If you have the tools needed for notching the ends of shelves (a saber saw or coping saw works well), you can easily make a double-sided bookshelf like this one. Two floor-to-ceiling 4 by 4s support the shelves, one from each end (the shelves sit on 1" dowels pushed through holes drilled at matching heights through both 4 by 4s). Fasten the 4 by 4s to the ceiling, using L-brackets as shown. Cut the dowels either the same width as the shelves or slightly shorter. Notch the ends of shelves (3½" by 3½" for milled 4 by 4s) and sand all edges lightly; then finish as desired.

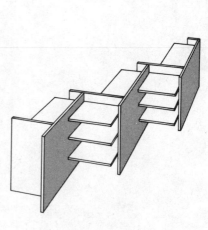

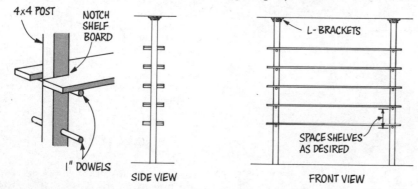

10 Divider shelving. This two-faced, zigzag shelving makes an excellent room divider. Although it takes up considerably more floor space than other shelving units, its low height keeps it visually unimposing. The back support for each shelf holds the side of the neighboring shelf, helping to minimize the amount of materials required. As a matter of fact, you can make the complete unit shown from two sheets of ¾" plywood and 75 screws. To make it, just cut out the pieces, slightly round corners and edges, and assemble them as shown. Design: John B. Brandon.

PLYWOOD LAYOUTS

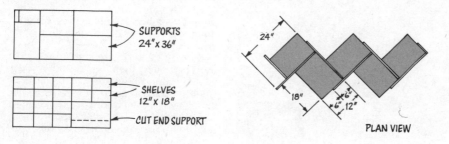

Built with drill, saw, lumber, & pegs

On this book's front cover is a closeup view of this peg-together shelving system. Because the entire unit is assembled using only wooden pegs, it is an ideal project for do-it-yourselfers who own only a few tools.

The unit is shown, on the cover, supporting large 2 by 12 shelves; here it is supporting 1 by 12 shelves. You can try several other variations. Shelves can be adjusted in height, in length, or you can even make them from other materials (see page 37). The unit can stretch along a wall for display or stand in the center of a room, serving double duty as a room divider. You can outfit it entirely with shelves, keeping the construction simple, or you can make and install one or more cabinets similar to the one shown. (The directions given here do not include making the cabinet — for information on how to make it, see page 38.) Design: Donald W. Vandervort.

TOOLS YOU'LL NEED

Here is a list of the tools you'll want to have on hand: pencil, measuring tape, combination square (optional but very handy), saw, electric drill, 1" spade or expansion bit, 9/16" bit, large nail or center punch, and hammer. A drill press is a very handy option. If you use an expansion bit, you'll need a screwdriver to adjust it.

MATERIALS

Because so many variations of size and structure exist with this modular-style shelving system, a precalculated materials list isn't offered. Instead, calculate the necessary materials from the following rules, after planning the size and appearance of the unit you'll want.

For a unit one shelf wide, you need four 8' 2 by 3s (to fit in a room with a standard 8' ceiling height). Be sure to choose lumber that is free of knots and defects. A unit two shelves wide needs six uprights; a three-shelf-wide unit needs eight; and so on.

These shelves are from 1 by 12 knotty pine ("Number 2 Pine"). They are 24" long, but you can make them up to 36" in length.

Two 12" 2 by 2s are needed for supporting each shelf. Unless the long (5⅝") support pegs are used to hold two shelf supports at the same level, you also need two 4⅛-inch-long 1-inch-diameter dowels for each shelf support (four per shelf). For each of these dowels, you need two ½-inch-diameter dowel pegs, 1½" long (eight per shelf). Last, one ceiling-pressure device (page 45) is required for each 2 by 3 upright.

HERE'S HOW

Difficult to make? Not at all. If you have the lumberyard cut the shelves to length, your only job is cutting and drilling the 2 by 3s, 2 by 2s, dowels, and pegs. Exercise your best talents when drilling the holes — these must be accurately placed and straight. If you don't have a drill press to help you drill straight, turn to page 22 for helpful suggestions.

1 Cut all of the pieces to size. The upright 2 by 3s are about 1" shorter than ceiling height. The 2 by 2 shelf supports are each 12" long. The 1-inch-diameter dowels are two different lengths: 5⅝" and 4⅛". The longer ones hold a support on each side of an upright (for neighboring shelves). Cut the ½" dowel pegs to 1½" lengths. Have the shelf boards cut to the exact length at the lumberyard (24" is a good size).

2 Mark for drilling the holes. Lay the 2 by 3s next to each other, butting them against something square, such as a wall. Beginning 10½" from one end

(that end will be the foot of the finished unit), mark for 1" holes every 6" along their lengths (you can mark four at a time, using a combination square as shown).

3 Set the combination square to exactly half the 2 by 3s' width (about 1¼") and mark the center of each hole-placement line that you made in step 2. Using

a large nail or pointed tool, punch a small hole at the center point for each hole.

4 Lay out the 1" holes on the 2 by 2s as shown in the sketch. The critical distance is *between* the holes, not from

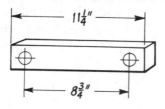

the holes to the ends of the 2 by 2. Measure or use the square to center the marks; then center punch them.

5 Mark and center punch the 1-inch-diameter dowel pegs as shown in the sketch. Be sure the marks are parallel.

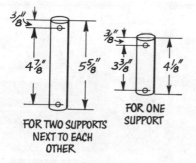

FOR TWO SUPPORTS NEXT TO EACH OTHER

FOR ONE SUPPORT

6 Drill the 1" holes. Before drilling, decide how you'll finish the unit. If you plan to paint or apply a surface-coating finish, make the holes slightly larger than the 1" dowel diameter. Using an expansion bit is advisable — you can make slight adjustments in its diameter. Drill a hole through a piece of

scrap and make sure all of the doweling can be pushed easily through the hole (doweling may vary slightly in diameter). Although you want the holes large enough to receive the dowels easily, don't make them so large that the dowels will fit loosely.

Drill the 1" holes through the 2 by 3s and 2 by 2s. These holes must be neat and straight. Methods for drilling straight and hints showing how to avoid splitting away the wood's backside are given on page 22.

7 Drill the 9/16" holes through the dowels, using a special holder such as the one shown on page 22.

8 Finish and assemble the unit. Sand the ends of the dowels and the rest of the shelving members; then add a finish (page 52). Attach a pressure device to the top of each 2 by 3 as shown

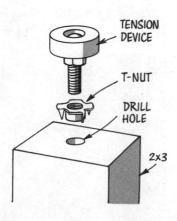

TENSION DEVICE

T-NUT

DRILL HOLE

2x3

(see more about these devices on page 45). Be sure to check the unit for level and plumb (page 16) as you set it up.

Display modules: esthetic & simple

Made to custom-fit your prized possessions and arranged to your liking, these handsome modules are sturdily formed from 2 by 12 lumber. Because of their strong construction, they don't need supporting backs — a very simple design requiring no special workshop savvy is the result. The only part of the project that takes patience and elbow grease is shaping the corners.

The instructions and materials list are for making one of the square modules. For variations and additional modules, change measurements and add to your materials list. The two modules shown housing stereo speakers are enclosed at the front by plywood panels with speakers mounted behind cutouts. Wood molding (1" by 1") rimming the inner side secures the panels to cabinets with glue and 5d nails. Speaker cloth then covers all. The interior shelves are ¼" smoked glass, purchased at a glass shop. Design: Rick Morrall.

Different arrangement of cabinets holds a TV set, creates a room divider.

TOOLS YOU'LL NEED

These are the necessary tools: saw, hammer or mallet, drill, ¼" bit, ¾" bit, measuring tape, compass, straightedge (combination square is excellent), pencil, rasp or belt sander, and sandpaper. Corner clamps are optional but very handy.

MATERIALS

Because the dimensions of these modules vary, the materials listed here are those needed for building one of the standard 24" (outside diameter) modules: two 21" lengths of 2 by 12, two 24" lengths of 2 by 12, 36" of ¾" softwood dowels, shelf pins, and glue.

HOW TO MAKE ONE SQUARE MODULE

First, pick out the clearest softwood planks you can find at your lumberyard (the examples here are redwood). If you don't have a power saw for cutting them to the exact length, have the lumberyard do the cutting for a small fee (be sure to give them exact measurements).

Finished softwood lumber almost always comes with rounded edges; you will need to trim these to make the edges square. If you don't have a jointer or tablesaw for this, ask the lumberyard

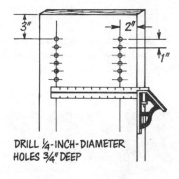

"FINISH" CORNERS COME SLIGHTLY ROUNDED FROM LUMBERYARD

TRIM SIDES UNTIL CORNERS ARE SHARP AND "SQUARE"

folks to do this job, too. Follow the steps below after the lumber is cut to exact lengths and properly surfaced.

1 Measure in 2" on the side pieces and drill ¼" holes about ¾" deep and 1" apart for adjustable metal shelf pins. Be sure to keep these in a straight line (see layout sketch).

DRILL ¼-INCH-DIAMETER HOLES ¾" DEEP

2 Sand all of the flat surfaces (but not the corners) before assembling. Be sure the two ends of the side 2 by 12s are perfectly square so they can form snug joints (trim slightly if necessary).

3 Glue the pieces together at right angles (corner clamps, like those shown in the photo above right, make the job easier). Let the glue dry. Drill three ¾"

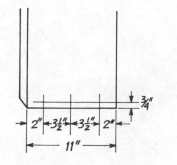

holes, all ¾" in from the top's ends. One hole should be centered across the lumber's width, the other two each about 2" in from the edges. Drill down about 2½" into the wood. Squeeze some glue around the inside perimeter

of each hole and pound in the 3-inch-long, ¾" dowels. Carefully trim off the dowels' extra ½" with a saw.

4 Mark a 1½-inch-radius quarter circle on the lumber's edges at each corner to outline rounded corners. Also draw lines 1½" in from the corner across top and side pieces to show the limits of the

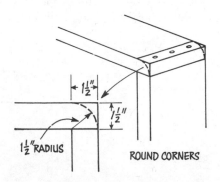

ROUND CORNERS

curves. Use a rasp or a power sander to round the corners, working downward with the wood grain. Sand the entire unit and finish as desired. This unit was treated with oil and a coat of wax.

Give hardware a flair

Track-and-bracket shelving hardware is strong, adjustable, and easy to assemble and mount. But the metal hardware screwed directly to the wall can often appear somewhat rough and unfinished. Shown here are ways to customize track-and-bracket supports by accenting or disguising them with wood. Either use the ideas as shown or adapt them to suit your needs.

You can buy the basic aluminum or steel hardware at most hardware stores or home-improvement centers in several colors and finishes. The vertical tracks come in lengths from 12" to 12'. The varying lengths of supporting brackets hold shelves from 4" to 20" wide. (You can use brackets that are slightly shorter than a shelf's width by drilling a ¼" hole or making a small notch in the underside of the shelf to accept the bracket's tip. This will help hide the bracket from view.)

For maximum stability, fasten the tracks to wall studs (see page 50). Screw in the top screw first, make sure the track is vertical by eye or by using a level or plumb bob (page 16), and then add the remaining screws.

Track-and-bracket shelving *hardware, available in hardware stores and home-improvement centers, is the key element of the designs on these two pages.*

Grooves *along lengths of 3" by 3" posts inset tracks for this system. Design: Edmund Ong, Architect.*

Wall of books *is simply a system of shelving brackets and standards. Cut verticals to fit the already-mounted horizontals. Design: Fred W. Taylor.*

Subdivided boxes *sit on brackets. Like the book wall shown at left, order of assembly is important. First screw standards to the wall and add brackets where you'll want shelves. Set the shelves on the brackets; then measure and cut the verticals to fit. Glue and nail them to the shelves. Design: Stuart Goforth, Architect.*

Kitchen counter *and shelf are supported by heavy-duty tracks, fitted into 1" by ¾" routed grooves in 3" by 3" redwood posts. Design: Edmund Ong, Architect.*

Freestanding bookshelf *has tracks mounted on 2 by 4 posts, faced toward wall. Pressure devices (page 45) secure it. Design: Stuart Goforth, Architect.*

Shelves fit in pregrooved plywood

Dozens of grooves in the plywood of this shelving unit provide support for adjustable shelves. And you don't have to cut a single groove — just buy the plywood (a type of exterior house siding) with the grooves already milled into it.

Several variations of the plywood are available. Its wood may be fir or redwood, its texture can be smooth or resawn, and its grooves can be on 4", 6", 8", 10", or 12" centers. The type used here is called "Texture 1-11." It is resawn redwood plywood with ⅜" grooves on 4" centers.

When buying panels, be sure both front and back sides are good looking — they both will be visible on the sides of the shelving unit. Avoid buying panels with a heavy preservative odor (outdoor siding is often treated). If you must buy treated panels, plan to let them air out for several weeks. Design: Donald Wm. MacDonald, AIA.

TOOLS YOU'LL NEED

Basic tools for this unit are a pencil, measuring tool, combination square, saw, drill, ⅛" bit, ¼" bit, hammer, nail-set or large nail, screwdriver, wrench, and finishing tools.

MATERIALS

This unit is made from the following materials: six 8' 2 by 3s; 31' of ½" by ¾" molding; one sheet of ⅜" A-B plywood; two sheets of ⅝" grooved plywood; six ¼" by 1½" hanger bolts, washers, and nuts; six ¼" by 1¼" screws; eight L-brackets with screws; white glue; ¾" corrugated fasteners; and 4d finish nails.

HERE'S HOW

Cutting the plywood to size can be a chore if you don't have the proper tools. (See additional cutting information on page 17.) To save time and make transporting the plywood easier, have the lumberyard make the major cuts.

Cut the plywood according to the diagram. Notice that one edge on the grooved plywood is made to overlap adjoining sheets; the other underlaps. Match those edges to the diagram. Cut off the shorter overlapping flange of the four 48" by 15½" panels (this cut edge will face down on the frames).

Also cut the 8' 2 by 3s down to 80⅜" for the vertical parts of the frames. Reduce the leftover block to 11" for the horizontals.

1 Assemble the three 2 by 3 frames, using glue and corrugated fasteners and checking each corner for "square." *Only use the fasteners where plywood will hide them.* Plywood will not cover them on the outer sides of the two outside frames. Don't worry about each joint's strength — the plywood will add the strength. Plan to put the panels with the best backside appearances on the unit's side frames.

2 Interlock a 32" and 48" panel (both are 15½" wide) on one of the frames, leaving the proper ⅜" groove at their intersection. The short top panel's squarely-cut edge should be flush with the frame's top. The pair's back edges should be flush with the frame's back edge; the front edge is inset ½". If the frame bows out at the middle, pull it in as you nail (use 4d finish nails and glue). Let the plywood fall short at the frame's bottom.

3 Use a shelf to line up the grooves of the next frame's panels with those on the frame you just finished. The photograph's view is from the frames' bottom side; notice how both panels fall short the same distance. If all grooves are not lined up precisely, shelves won't sit level or fit properly. Don't forget

that the center frame is covered on both sides: when applying the panels to the second side, lay the frame across a couple of blocks so the finished side won't be marred or soiled. Repeat the same procedures for the last frame's panels.

4 Support the frames on their back edges by sliding shelves in top and bottom grooves. Miter and nail ½" by ¾" molding to the front and side edges of the top panel (use 3d finish nails and glue). Set the top in position and tack it temporarily to one outside frame. Check for "square" and drill two ⅛" holes through the top into one end frame — one hole 4" from the back, one 4" from the front, both 1" in from the top's side edge.

Remove the top, turn the hanger bolts into the holes until about 1" protrudes (spin on a nut, turn the bolt into the wood with a wrench, and then remove the nut). Enlarge the top's holes with a ¼" bit, push the frame's hanger bolts through these holes, add washers and nuts, and tighten. Move over to the center frame, tack the top to it, install hanger bolts the same way, and repeat the same procedures on the other end frame.

5 Stand up the unit and lean the back panel against the frame backsides with its grooves forward and the overlapping flange at top. Slide bottom shelves out the back about ½", as shown in the small sketch, and fit them into the back panel's matching groove to insure proper alignment. Temporari-

ly tack the panel there. Make sure the unit is standing straight and the back is "square" with the frames. Bottom shelves should be snug but not stuck in their grooves. Then drill ⅛" holes and countersink screws.

6 Face the front edges of shelves with ½" by ¾" molding (use glue and 4d finish nails). Let the molding overlap at the sides, as shown. Set all finishing nails in the unit below the surface. Fill holes, sand, and finish as desired.

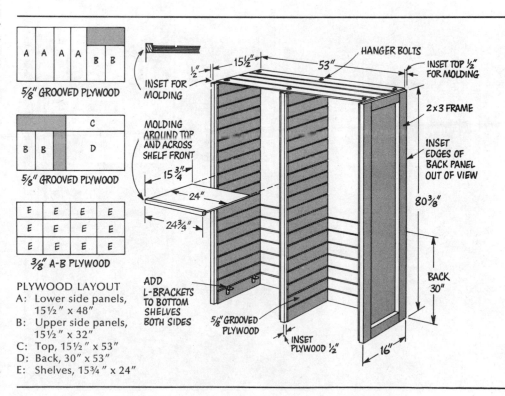

PLYWOOD LAYOUT
A: Lower side panels, 15½" x 48"
B: Upper side panels, 15½" x 32"
C: Top, 15½" x 53"
D: Back, 30" x 53"
E: Shelves, 15¾" x 24"

Wall system is adjustable, collapsible

This shelving unit sturdily holds books, records, music equipment, and even a seat. And when it's time to change residence or rearrange the room, it easily dismantles, leaving no trace on the walls or ceiling.

The unit's structural simplicity both adds to its attractiveness and makes it fairly easy to build. It needn't stand against the wall either; it works equally well as a room divider.

The desk and tape storage units are simple plywood boxes (see page 38) designed to fit between the shelves. The fronts of the two tape-storage boxes open on piano hinges. Lid support hinges hold the desk front horizontal when it's in use. Design: Pat Noda, AIA.

Small pegs *fitted between vertical 1 by 4s support ¾" dowels; the dowels in turn support the 1 by 10 shelves.*

TOOLS YOU'LL NEED

The tools necessary for making this pegged-together unit are a pencil, a measuring tool, C-clamps, a drill with a ¼" bit, a saw, a hammer, and finishing tools.

MATERIALS

Because you can make the unit to any size, required materials depend upon how big you make it. Reduce the design into basic elements to determine materials. One of the 8' uprights (for standard ceiling height) requires about 36' of 1 by 4, and forty 2½-inch-long ¼" dowel pegs. The shelves are 1 by 10s — you can vary the length slightly (the ones shown are 36" long). To hold each shelf, you need two 20-inch-long supports of ¾" doweling. Each upright will require two ceiling-pressure devices (page 45).

Desk and cabinets *rest on shelves. Desk is simply a box cabinet with a drop-down door that becomes a work surface.*

HERE'S HOW

Drilling holes straight is the toughest part of making this system. If you don't have a drill press for doing this, consult page 22 for some helpful hints.

Cut the vertical 1 by 4s slightly shorter than ceiling height to allow room for ceiling-pressure devices. Cut the rest of the pieces according to the materials list.

1 Clamp two 1 by 4 verticals together, flush on all edges. Beginning 12" from what will be the bottom end, center and drill a ¼" hole every 3" along the boards' lengths through both boards, stopping about 12" from the top end. Put a scrap beneath the boards so the bit doesn't split away the wood as it penetrates. (When you drill these holes through the other verticals, be sure they are at the same dimensions so shelves will sit level.)

2 Unclamp the two verticals and carefully pound the dowels into the holes of one of the 1 by 4s. Align the other 1 by 4 over the pegs.

3 Starting at one end, fit the pegs into their respective holes as shown. Once you get a few in at one end, clamp that end of the two 1 by 4s together with a C-clamp so the pegs you've fitted won't pop out as you fit further pegs. Stick ¾" blocks between the boards to keep an even ¾" space between them, and, if necessary, use a mallet or a hammer against a block (so you don't mar the surface) to tap the uprights together. When pegs are all in place and the spacing between the 1 by 4s is uniformly ¾", sand any protruding peg ends flush. Repeat these processes with the other pairs. (Again—be sure pegs will be at the same levels when you stand up the verticals.)

4 Glue and dowel (2 pegs at each corner) the 1 by 4 crosspieces in place at top and bottom, letting them extend 1⅝" as shown. Sand protruding ends of these two pegs flush. Repeat the procedures for the other uprights, add ceiling-pressure devices to the tops, finish as desired (page 52), and set up the unit in your room.

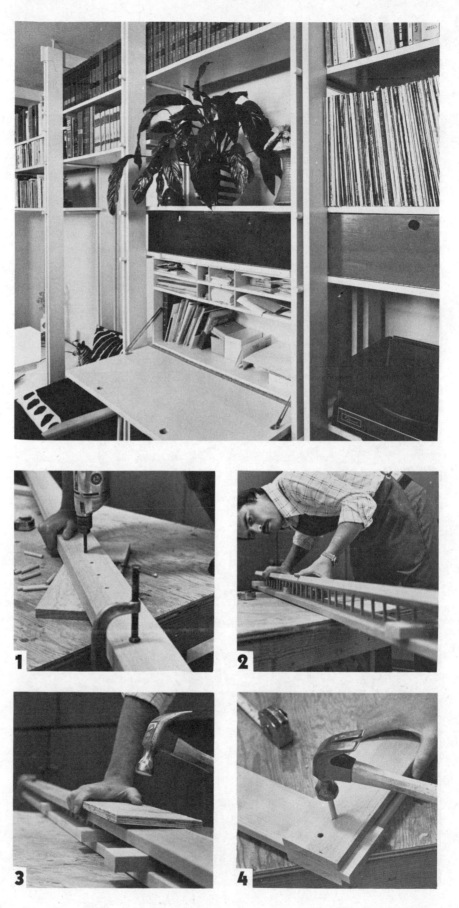

Strong, rustic, & easy to make

Rough redwood and dowels create the character of this bold bookcase. Offset here against an adobe wall, the bookcase offers a feeling of strength and rustic simplicity. But the real beauty of this design is the fact that it is very simple to construct and requires a minimum of materials.

The uprights are rough redwood 2 by 10s. Rough lumber, although cheaper than finished lumber, is generally not recommended for cabinets and shelving — it is splintery and, because it carries more moisture than finished wood, may warp after the project is built. In the case of this project, there are no tight-fitting joints that would tattle on slight warpage, and the rough wood is used where it doesn't need to be smooth. If the wood is a bit too rough, you can buff off some of the splinters with sandpaper. Design: Roger Flanagan.

TOOLS AND MATERIALS

The only tools required to make this bookshelf are a pencil, measuring tool, saw, drill, 1" bit, mallet or hammer, screwdriver, and finishing tools.

The necessary materials will depend upon the size of the unit you build — it needn't be the same size as this one. This unit required four 7' rough redwood 2 by 10s, fifteen 36-inch-long 1 by 10s, and about 21' of 1-inch-diameter hardwood doweling. You'll also need about a dozen L-brackets for steps 4 and 5.

HERE'S HOW

Building the bookcase is a relatively simple job. You need only cut the pieces to size, drill holes, insert dowels, and secure the unit in place. Before construction, these shelves were stained to match the redwood uprights.

1 Cut the 2 by 10s, shelves, and dowels to length. The 2 by 10s should be about ¼" shorter than ceiling height. The shelves are 36" long and the 72 dowel pegs 3½" long. If you don't have a good power saw, you may want to measure the exact length to cut the 2 by 10s, figure the number of shelves for the unit, and ask them to cut these boards at the lumberyard. Remove any shagginess around the cut ends of the wood with sandpaper.

2 Mark the 2 by 10s (refer to sample plan), and drill the 1-inch-diameter holes. Lay a piece of scrap wood beneath the holes you're drilling so the wood's backside won't break away as the drill pierces (see more about drilling on page 21). Be sure to drill the holes straight.

3 Knock the 3½" dowels into the holes using a mallet (or softening the blows with a wood block between a hammer and the dowel). Center the dowels so that they stick out from each side an equal length.

4 Figure roughly where you want the bookcase to stand. Because it has no back, it must be fastened either to the wall or to the ceiling using L-brackets. Since the wall behind this unit was masonry, it was easier to secure the unit to the ceiling. First, find the location of wall studs or ceiling joists (page 50), and then plan to fasten at least two of the uprights directly to these. (The longer the L-brackets are, the more the chance of hitting a stud or joist.) If you have room, lay the uprights on their back edges, roughly in position and extended out from the wall. You can use the shelves to space them properly. If you don't have room, you'll need to have someone help you by holding them in place as you space them.

Before raising the uprights, get a level ready (or some other means of "plumbing" the uprights—see page 16), and a chair or something else to stand on (if you'll be fastening to the ceiling). Also stick a pencil and an L-bracket in your pocket.

Stand up one of the 2 by 10s that will be fastened to a stud or joist, level it, mark the L-bracket's placement on the 2 by 10, lay the 2 by 10 back down, fasten the L-bracket to it, stand it up again, and then screw the bracket to the stud or joist. Follow the same procedures for the remaining 2 by 10s, using the shelves as spacers. Use hollow-wall fasteners where you can't fasten into studs or joists (see pages 50, 51).

5 Slide the shelves in place and connect the undersides of the lower shelves to the 2 by 10s with smaller L-brackets. This will prevent the uprights from pulling away from the shelves at the bottom of the bookcase.

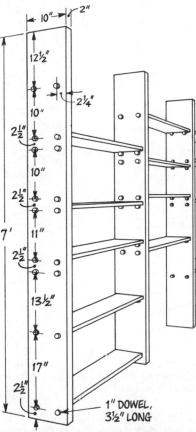

Plastic pipe system

This contemporary shelving design brings plastic sprinkler pipe in from the cold. Plastic pipe's workability, light weight, and very low cost all pay off in making this portable, adjustable bookshelf unit an outstanding project.

Simplicity is the key. The lines are simple, the components are few, and building it is a breeze, using only a tape measure, a saw, and a power drill.

Totally adjustable, the system works along a wall, turns corners, or serves as a room divider. Raise or lower the shelves simply by loosening wing nuts and sliding the supports up or down. The unit's modular adjustability extends to all sorts of alternatives (see "Alternatives" at right). And not one screw or nail penetrates the ceiling or wall — the unit is easily wedged between ceiling and floor as shown. This makes it ideal for apartment dwellers.

TOOLS YOU'LL NEED

As already mentioned, tools needed are few: a pencil, a measuring tool, a saw (handsaw is adequate, especially if you have the plywood shelves cut at the lumberyard), and an electric drill with a ¼" bit and a 1" spade bit (or an adjustable bit).

MATERIALS

This unit required eight 8' lengths of white 1" (outside diameter) "Schedule A" plastic sprinkler pipe; about 85' of 1 by 2 (be sure it's a full ¾" thick); one sheet of ⅜" A-C plywood; forty-six each ¼" by 2" carriage bolts, washers, and wing nuts.

HERE'S HOW

As you can see from the numbered steps below, making this unit is a simple, four-step process.

1 Cut the plastic pipe supports with a standard handsaw (the finer the teeth, the better) to measurements ¼" shorter than the dimension between your ceiling and floor. In most houses and apartments, the standard ceiling is 8' above the floor.

Then cut the pairs of supports from the 1 by 2s. For the unit shown, you'll need 22 pieces 16" long and 24 pieces 28" long.

2 Holding each pair flush together, drill a ¼" hole 2½" from each end (and centered) as shown. By dropping a bolt through the first holes before drilling the second, you can keep the holes perfectly aligned.

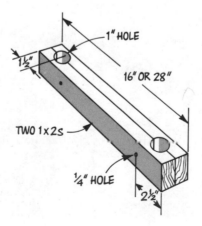

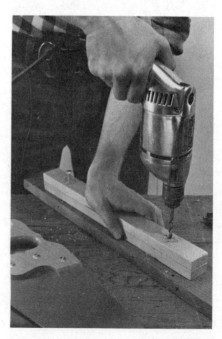

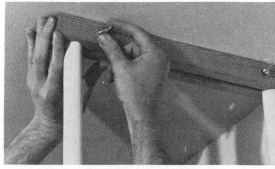

Push *top supports against ceiling; then tighten wing nuts. This wedges shelving unit between ceiling and floor.*

3 Bolt each pair of supports together, turn them on edge, and bore a 1" hole 1½" from each end, centered in the groove, keeping a piece of scrap beneath so the holes won't splinter away. Milling of 1 by 2s can differ, so

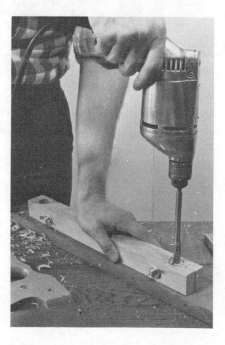

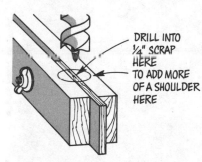

DRILL INTO ¼" SCRAP HERE

TO ADD MORE OF A SHOULDER HERE

check to be sure a full ¼" of wood is left on the outer side of these holes. If this wood is not available, tighten a ¼" scrap between the two supports and drill into it instead (as illustrated).

4 Finish the materials. Clean dirt and ink marks off the plastic pipe with lacquer thinner, alcohol, or scouring cleanser. Fill the edges and defects in the plywood shelves with spackling compound, sand them, and paint them.

The redwood shelf supports shown were sanded and given a clear finish.

When assembling the unit, carefully measure the height of each end of each support from the floor before tightening to keep shelves level (don't overtighten).

Alternatives. Using the concept of this system as a guide, you can try modifications. Instead of plastic tubing, you might try shiny aluminum tubing or electrical conduit. Add molding to the shelves' edges or completely change shelf sizes or materials — solid board, particle board, or glass will work (if you choose glass, check with your dealer on appropriate sizes, be very careful when setting the shelves up, and be sure the shelves rest on *at least* ¼" of wood at both ends). Instead of wing nuts, you might like to countersink regular nuts or use machine bolts with T-nuts.

When altering the given design, you need to keep in mind a couple of structural thoughts. Avoid spanning the shelves over distances greater than 30", and, if you alter shelf placement, just be sure each set of pipes is joined at two or three well-spaced points in both directions so the unit is tied together firmly as a whole.

Recycled storage

Take a tired-out box or barrel and give it new life. Here are some interesting ways to turn something that looks useless into useful storage. You'd be surprised at how many materials of this sort are free for the asking, too. Four out of the six storage ideas shown were made from free materials; the fiber drums were purchased for a minimal fee (listed in the phone book under "Barrels and Drums"), and the old post-office box was discovered in an antique hunt. Perhaps these few ideas can help spark your imagination into creating equally interesting storage answers from recycled materials.

Soda-pop case *is sectioned with cubbyhole shelves that are just the right size for holding spice bottles, small jars.*

Wooden boxes, *cleaned up and stacked, offer rustic — and free — storage.*

Shadowbox display/storage for toys consists of assorted boxes glued randomly to plywood, framed by molding.

Cardboard mailing tubes, cut and stacked between shelves, make padded holders for storing wine bottles.

Antique mailbox returns to usefulness, proudly storing small knick knacks.

Fiber drums become gaily-decorated toy/storage containers with sturdy metal lids. Available in several sizes, they are ideal for storing bulky objects.

Sophisticated boxes

On the preceding two pages, you can see how worn-out boxes can be turned into useful storage. Here, that theme is taken one step further — for these projects, you make the boxes. Although all of the storage units on these two pages are of different shapes, sizes, and materials, they have one thing in common — they're easily made from homemade boxes.

Made to fit their contents, these resawn redwood storage boxes jut and recess from each other, forming a visually exciting display-storage system. (See a portion of this unit in color on the back cover.)

The entire system is made from simple boxes of resawn redwood siding that share a common back: 3 sheets of resawn redwood plywood. Glue and nail (6d finish nails) the boxes together individually; then screw the largest ones to the back (the smaller ones can then be set in place). You may want to screw some of the boxes to each other, as well.

Screwing the boxes to the back is somewhat difficult. You may prefer trying a variation: give each box its own back and then stack them, bolting or screwing them to each other. This way, they are also easier to rearrange. The wall will show through where no boxes are positioned.

Where one width of the resawn siding isn't wide enough to give the proper depth to a box, use two or three widths, joining them at the corners as shown below. Design: Greg Smith, The Just Plain Smith Company.

STAGGER NARROW & WIDE PANELS

Here are some elegant boxes made for stacking. These boxes are made from ¾ " A-A grade plywood, assembled with 4d nails, white glue, and simple butt joints. To soften the angularity and to hide the butt joints, mask the open sides of each box with a ⅛ " hardboard facing that has curved corners. (Cut out the inside of 16″ by 32″ hardboard panels with a saber saw, coping saw, or router.) Five of the boxes have inserted backs covered with fabric. Small light bulbs help illuminate the contents of each module (wood spacers ¼ " thick leave enough room between stacked boxes for wiring). The entire unit rests on a 13″ by 58″ dark-stained base of 2 by 6s and is crowned by a similar frame to hide wiring: Design: Bill Nilsen.

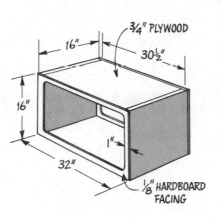

Mahogany frames make up this shelving system. The entire unit is made from backless square and rectangular boxes made from ¾ " by 10″ mahogany boards. Corners of each were simply butt joined, glued, and screwed together (1¾ " screws). Countersink the heads of the screws and plug each hole with a mahogany plug (see plug cutter on page 33). Sand the unit carefully and give it a clear finish (page 52). Design: Art Swindle.

Boxes bolted together form a freestanding storage unit. Seven boxes, when bolted together as shown, will give you fourteen surfaces on which to store your possessions (seventeen if you use the floor beneath the boxes, too). If you add strong ½ " backs to each box, they can serve to help move things when you disassemble the unit. Design: Tom Clements.

BOLT BOXES TOGETHER, AS SHOWN HERE, OR TRY A VARIATION OF YOUR OWN

Bolt boxes to wooden 1 by 2s or aluminum bars. This, like the system discussed above, will give you considerably more storage than the number of boxes you make, saving materials, time, and effort. Five boxes will give you ten surfaces for putting things on, eleven if you use the floor space beneath the center box. Butt join, glue, and nail the corners of the boxes together and then add backs to them. Design: John B. Brandon.

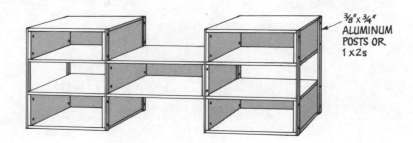

⅜″ x ¾″ ALUMINUM POSTS OR 1 x 2s

Box cubes for storage or play

The furniture in this child's room consists of a bed, a tiny chair, and a dozen gaily painted plywood boxes. That's all. The modular boxes (they're 16" cubes) are easy to build, inexpensive, and very versatile. They stack together to form useful bookcases, room dividers, wall storage cabinets, desks, and other prosaic things that parents think of. And they go together to make caves, tunnels, airplanes, houses, trains, and other wondrous things that children think of.

Although the boxes are sturdy, they're so lightweight a young child can lift one. To make the boxes more fun yet still usable for storage, some have large holes — two round or rectangular holes in opposite sides or a large round hole in one side.

Box blocks can be both fun and functional, depending upon how they're stacked.

TOOLS AND MATERIALS

The boxes have ¼" plywood sides (lauan plywood is excellent), joined together with aluminum corner moldings (#3006 of the do-it-yourself aluminum). You can make seven of the cubes from two sheets of plywood. For the same seven cubes, you'll need about 38' of the aluminum molding. Glue or wall-paneling mastic will also be needed.

You can build the boxes with only hand tools, but a radial-arm saw or table saw makes the job much easier (unless you have the plywood panels cut at the lumberyard). You can cut the aluminum right along with the plywood if you use a power saw, as shown, but you'll need a hacksaw to cut it if you must do it by hand. For cutting the holes, you'll need a keyhole saw or saber saw. You'll also need a hammer for nailing small brads, a file for smoothing cut edges of aluminum, and finishing tools.

HERE'S HOW

Cut the side panels an even 16" high but only 15¼" wide (to leave room for the corner posts). Cut the bottoms *approximately* 15⅜" square (before cutting, double-check this dimension on an assembled box; it can vary slightly). Glue sides into corner posts with white glue or a wall-paneling mastic. Use white glue liberally; use mastic sparingly. Secure the bottom to the sides with glue and ¾" decorative-head brads. File down all sharp corner post edges.

You can cut the large holes before or after assembly. If necessary, strengthen the plywood above the holes with strips of hardwood, glued to the inside. Then just paint the cubes the cheery colors your children like.

AN ALTERNATIVE

If you can't find those aluminum corner posts, you can make the cubes like these. Cut them as shown in the diagram from ½" plywood (as with the other cubes, you can make three cubes from one 4' by 8' sheet of plywood; seven cubes from two sheets). Use glue and 1d finishing nails to hold the simple butt joints. Then cut the holes in the sides of the cubes with a saber saw or keyhole saw; putty and sand all corners, edges, and joints; and paint the cubes. Design: Harry & Helen Som.

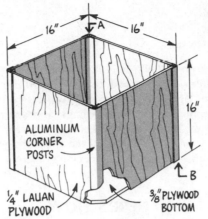

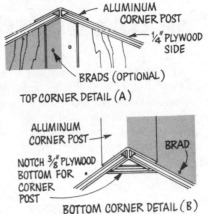

TOP CORNER DETAIL (A)

BOTTOM CORNER DETAIL (B)

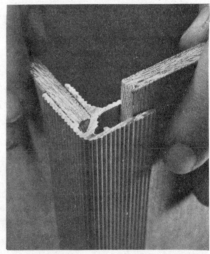

Aluminum *can be cut along with plywood if you use a radial-arm or table saw. Choose an old blade.*

Glue plywood sides *into aluminum corner posts. Wall paneling mastic adhesive, used sparingly, forms a sure bond.*

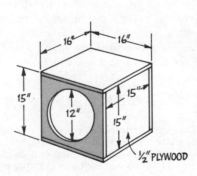

The bag board

Stuffed with scarves and mittens in an entry hall, exhibiting magazines in a reading area, or overflowing with office paraphernalia, the bag board provides an inexpensive, decorative means of storing things on a wall. It consists of a piece of plywood or particle board, four canvas bags, and some hooks — period. And for someone who's handy with a needle and thread, making it is as easy as sewing on buttons. (You can also see this storage board in color on the back cover.) Design: Donald Wm. MacDonald, AIA.

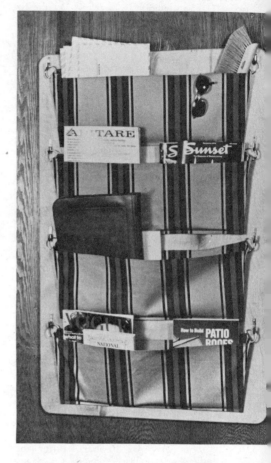

TOOLS YOU'LL NEED

The main tool you'll need for this project is a regular sewing machine, equipped with a heavy-duty needle and set for 10 to 12 stitches per inch. Other tools include a pencil, measuring tool, compass, scissors, curve-cutting saw, drill with a screw-pilot bit, and screwdriver. You can have the board cut to size at the lumberyard (or hunt around for precut pieces); if you don't, you'll need a saw for cutting it.

MATERIALS

The board is cut from a half sheet of plywood (particle board is fine). You'll also need 3 yards of canvas, a spool of polyester thread, eight hooks with screws, eight 2" rings, and about six 3" screws for attaching the board to the wall.

HERE'S HOW

You can buy the materials for the board and bags at the same time, but make the bags before attaching the hooks to the board. When sewing the bags, backstitch at the beginning and end of each stitching line for strength. Before stitching each seam, either baste, pin baste, or press each turned seam (use a pressing cloth when ironing).

1 Make patterns from paper according to the sketch shown and lay the patterns on the finish side of the canvas. If stripes or other patterns decorate your canvas, align them so they'll match. Cut out the material.

2 Lay a front panel on a back panel, both appearance sides up. Fold under ½" of both panels along the lower edge, baste or press, and double-stitch along the seam, running the first row of stitching about ⅛" up from the edge.

Plastic wall organizer

Although plastic storage boards sell in stores for as much as $40, you can make this one for about $5. It's great for organizing office supplies by a desk, holding knickknacks near a worktable, or storing kitchen paraphernalia next to a counter. All you do is embed halved plastic kitchenware in polyester resin on a hardboard backing framed with molding.

You can make the board any size and affix practically any shape object of plastic or wood. Just design it around the things you'll want to store.

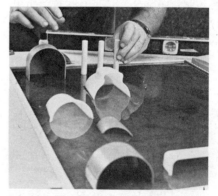

Level *backing board before pouring resin to 3/16" depth. Quickly insert holders.*

TOOLS YOU'LL NEED

Necessary tools are a pencil, measuring tool, saw, drill with screw-pilot bit, hammer, level, mixing stick and measuring container for the resin, sandpaper, and paint brush.

MATERIALS

The size and shape of your storage board will determine the necessary materials. You need ¼" tempered hardboard for backing; enough ½" L-shaped molding to circle its perimeter; polyester casting resin (about 1 quart for a 16" by 22" board); miscellaneous rigid plastic kitchenware, plastic flower pots, dowels, and so forth; a handful of brads; glue; and a pint of high-gloss enamel.

center seam. This will keep its front from drooping when it holds magazines or other tall articles.

6 Attach rings. Fold the protruding flap through a ring and pin the flap to the back canvas panel. Leave it

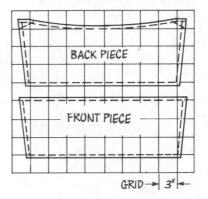

PATTERN FOR CANVAS POCKETS

BACK PIECE

FRONT PIECE

GRID → 3" ←

3 Finish the top edges of the two panels by folding under ¼" and stitching about ⅛" in from the folded edges of each.

4 Fold under ½" of one of the side edges (both panels together) and stitch it like the bottom seam. End the

stitching at the top of the front section; then backstitch for strength. Do the same on the other side edge.

5 Depending upon how you plan to use the bags, you may want to divide each bag into two pockets with a

pinned until you've tested the bag by hanging it from the hooks — you may have to adjust the angle to get the stress on the flap equally distributed. Once tested, stitch it several times. Duplicate the preceding procedures for the other three bags.

7 Cut the plywood or particle board to size. Mark a 1½" radius on the corners using a compass; then cut around the lines with a curve-cutting saw (page 19). Sand all edges. Lay out the hooks according to the illustration, test their placement with the bags and rings, and screw them in place.

8 Finish the board as desired. Locate the wall studs in the wall (see page 50) and, according to their placement, drill holes behind the bags for 3" screws. Attach the board to the wall studs and enjoy your new wall storage board.

HERE'S HOW

Making the storage board is easy enough for anyone to do.

1 Cut the backing from ¼" tempered hardboard; then frame it with ½", L-shaped corner molding to make a narrow lip (fasten it with glue and brads). Use a saw to cut the rigid plastic kitchenware and other holders in half and sand their edges smooth.

2 Lay the holders, pegs, and such on the backing, mark their locations, and remove them. Mix a batch of polyester casting resin. Carefully level the backing board; then pour the resin to a 3/16" depth. Quickly set all pieces in place. Tap them to seat them firmly. When the resin dries thoroughly, sand the surface lightly and finish with high-gloss enamel. To attach it to wall studs (page 50), you can drill screw holes through the board.

STORAGE BOARDS 83

From one sheet of plywood

This adjustable shelf-and-desk combination has several features worth considering. First of all, it can be cut from one sheet of plywood. Second, making it requires very few tools; third, the design is adjustable; and fourth, the unit can be dismantled in minutes using only a screwdriver. Although the unit shown was given a clear polyurethane finish, you could paint or stain it. Design: Don Ryan.

TOOLS AND MATERIALS

As already mentioned, the tools and materials needed for building this unit are few. You'll need a pencil, measuring tape, saw, drill wtih ¾" and 3/16" bits, screwdriver, and finishing tools. Make the unit from one sheet of ¾" A-A grade plywood and about thirty-five Number 10 stove bolts (1½"), countersinking washers, and nuts. A piece of ⅛" hardboard can be tacked to the structure's back for added lateral strength.

HERE'S HOW

Unless you have a table saw or radial-arm saw, ask the lumberyard attendant to make the major cut across the middle of the plywood. Then cut the pieces according to the diagram, sand the edges smooth, and slightly round the corners.

1 Drill the ¾" and 3/16" holes through all of the pieces as illustrated. The holes through the ends of the shelves make them adjustable.

2 Set the two side pieces next to each other on their back edges and bolt the work surface to each side. Then bolt the top piece in place, followed first by the large bottom shelf and then by the remaining shelves.

3 Stand the unit up. If you wish to attach a back, do so (the back of the unit shown was covered with decorative paper first). The unit is now ready to finish and use.

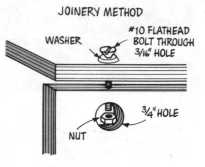

JOINERY METHOD

WASHER
#10 FLATHEAD BOLT THROUGH 3/16" HOLE
NUT
¾" HOLE

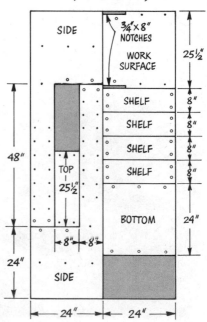

PLYWOOD LAYOUT
(¾" A-A PLYWOOD)

SIDE
¾" × 8" NOTCHES
WORK SURFACE
25½"
SHELF — 8"
SHELF — 8"
SHELF — 8"
SHELF — 8"
48"
TOP 25½"
BOTTOM — 24"
24"
8" 8"
SIDE
24"
24" 24"

Pop-together shelf system

Inspired by children's Tinker Toys, this pop-together shelving system is surprisingly strong and versatile. And if you have a table saw and drill press, it is an easy project to make (this is one of the few projects in this book that practically demands the use of sophisticated power tools for good results). The structure can be proportioned to fit any needs (for example, spans could be shorter to support heavier loads). It's made of 5⁄8″ hardwood dowels plugged into octagonal hubs cut from 4 by 4s. Shelves of 1⁄4″ tempered hardboard rest on the horizontal dowels. Design: Jim Plunkett.

Octagonal hub *receives dowels from ten directions. Diagonal dowels strengthen.*

TOOLS AND MATERIALS

For the unit shown, you'll need a pencil, measuring tool, table saw, drill press, 5⁄8″ spade bit, file, and coping saw. Necessary materials will depend upon the size of the unit you make. The structure is made of 5⁄8″ hardwood dowels plugged into octagonal hubs cut from 4 by 4s. Shelves of 1⁄4″ tempered hardboard rest on the horizontal dowels.

HERE'S HOW

Before beginning work, file a 5⁄8″ spade bit so it tapers slightly towards the point. This way, it can drill tapered holes in the hubs that will hold the dowels snugly.

1 For the hubs, use a table saw to rip the edges of a 4 by 4 at 45° angles, forming an octagon with 1⅜″ faces. Then cut off 1½-inch-thick slices.

2 Using a drill press (or drilling *very* straight with a hand drill), make holes ¾″ deep in each of the eight faces and in the center of the hub (for this hole, drill halfway through from both sides).

3 Cut dowels to the length you want. Then, with a coping saw, cut 1-inch-deep saw grooves in a cross pattern in the ends of each dowel so they can compress slightly as they are pushed into their holes.

4 Cut the hardboard shelves to fit your structure and notch them where they meet the hubs. Sand and finish all parts (page 52).

A triad of cabinet modules

Rounded corners, simple lines, and visible hardware flavor these cabinet modules with an accent of contemporary European design. Fitted with drawers or shelves and doors, they're not only visually pleasing — they work hard to provide storage.

The modules shown act as a bedroom chest of drawers, but you can use them any number of ways — for den storage, a dining room buffet, or even in the workshop. You don't have to stick with the given plans. Line them up or separate them. Make all three, just two, or only one. And if you decide you don't need drawers, make the work twice as easy by installing shelves and a door instead (like the module in the center). If you do make the modules different, just remember to make the required changes in the list of materials and the layouts.

As you can see in the list of required tools, a saber saw is optional. For this project, the saber saw is more than an option: it's a blessing. Used with a guide, you can cut those plywood panels much straighter and faster with a saber saw than with a handsaw. And when rounding all those corners, the saber saw really shines.

TOOLS AND MATERIALS

Tools necessary for making the modules include a pencil, measuring tool, compass, square, saw (saber saw is good option), drill, 5/16" bit, 1/8" bit (or screw-pilot bits), screwdriver, hammer, nailset or large nail, and finishing tools.

Materials for this project are two full sheets of 3/4" A-D plywood, one sheet of 1/2" A-D plywood, two sheets of 1/4"

hardboard, 9' of clear 2 by 2 for corner supports, 10' of 1/2" by 3/4" molding for drawer supports (more if you don't cut dadoes in drawer sides), eighteen 1" screws for attaching backs, twelve 1 1/2" screws for attaching front kick plates, twenty-four 2 1/2" by 5/16" carriage bolts, nuts, and washers. Miscellaneous supplies include extra molding for fastening the cabinet backs, butt hinges, shelf support pegs, white glue, and 3d finishing nails.

HERE'S HOW

Cut out the plywood as shown in the diagram. If possible, have the lumberyard make some of the major cuts. The measurements given are full measurements — be sure to allow for the saw blade's width (cut on the waste side of the cutting line). To simplify measuring, delay rounding the corners until step 4. If you won't be making the drawers, adjust your materials and measurements accordingly. Full instructions for making these types of drawers and installing them on side runners are given on pages 46-48. Methods of supporting shelves within a cabinet are on page 45; look on page 42 for information on hinges and doors.

1 Prepare the 2 by 2s. Cut six pieces, each 17 1/2" long. Center a mark 3 3/4" in from each end and drill 5/16" holes straight through (see information on drilling straight on page 22). Check the first two holes for accuracy; then use that 2 by 2 as a guide for duplicating the holes through the others (notice the bolt, dropped through first set of holes to maintain proper alignment).

2 Drill side panels. Lay one side panel good-face down with a scrap beneath where you'll be drilling. (That way, when you drill, you won't splinter away the good side.) At the two corners that will meet the cabinet's top, measure and mark 2 1/4" in from the side panel's front and back edges. Set the 2 by 2 between those two marks and inset it about 1/16" down from the panel's top edge, with the pre-drilled holes facing the panel (see photo). Is it lined up and square? If so, hold it firmly and use the two holes as guides for drilling matching holes through the side panel. After drilling the first hole, drop a bolt through to hold that end in place. Drill the second hole; then bolt the 2 by 2 in place.

3 Drill top panels. Prop a top and side panel together as shown. Make two marks on the top panel: both 3/4" from the side edge, one 7" from the front edge, the other 7" from back edge. Align the top so its front and back edges are flush with the side panel's edges. Hold the top's side edge snugly against the side panel's 1/16" recess and drill a 5/16" hole through both top and 2 by 2 at each of the marks. Again, drop a bolt through the first set of holes before going on to the second. When both are drilled, bolt the panels together. Repeat this procedure for each top-to-side corner joint.

4 Round the corners. Using a pencil, number and label the various pieces so you know what fits where. Then dis-

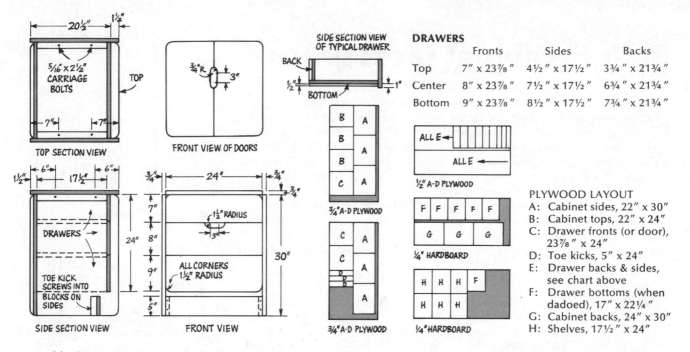

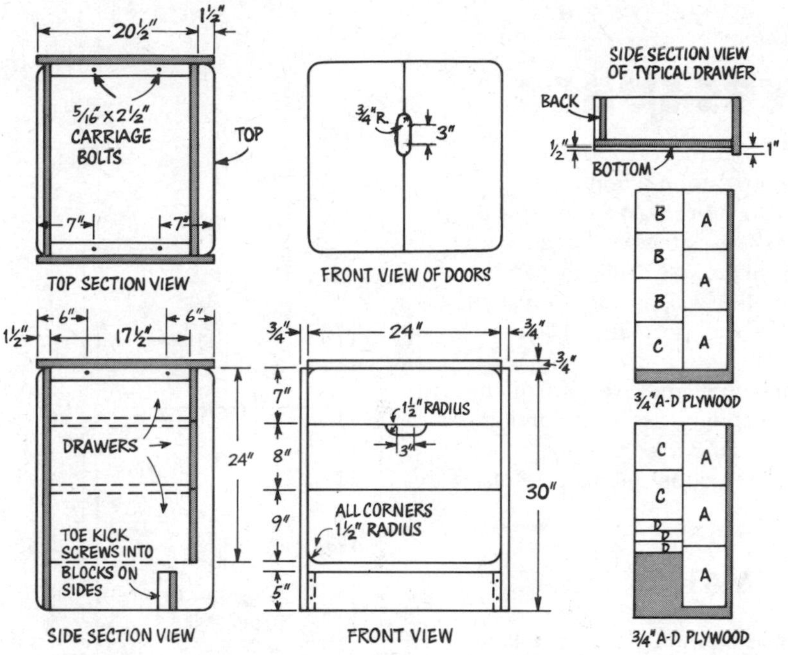
20½"
1½"
5/16 x 2½" CARRIAGE BOLTS
TOP
7"
7"
TOP SECTION VIEW
¾"R
3"
FRONT VIEW OF DOORS
SIDE SECTION VIEW OF TYPICAL DRAWER
BACK
½"
1"
BOTTOM
1½"
6"
17½"
6"
24"
DRAWERS
TOE KICK SCREWS INTO BLOCKS ON SIDES
SIDE SECTION VIEW
¾"
24"
¾"
¾"
7"
8"
9"
5"
1½" RADIUS
3"
ALL CORNERS 1½" RADIUS
30"
FRONT VIEW
B
A
B
A
B
C
A
¾" A-D PLYWOOD
C
A
C
A
D
D
D
A
¾" A-D PLYWOOD

DRAWERS

	Fronts	Sides	Backs
Top	7" x 23⅞"	4½" x 17½"	3¾" x 21¾"
Center	8" x 23⅞"	7½" x 17½"	6¾" x 21¾"
Bottom	9" x 23⅞"	8½" x 17½"	7¾" x 21¾"

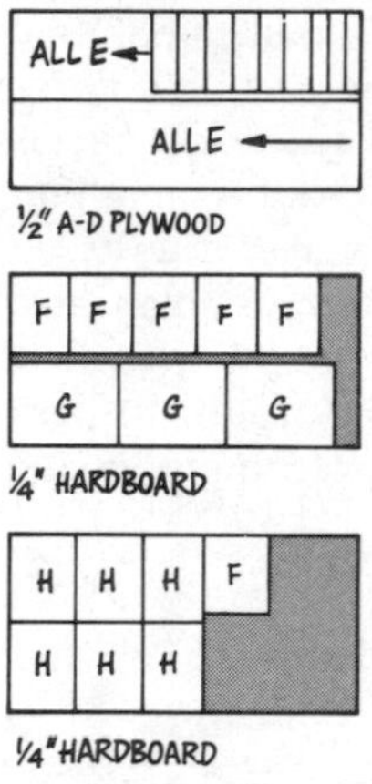
ALL E
ALL E
½" A-D PLYWOOD
F F F F F
G G G
¼" HARDBOARD
H H H F
H H H
¼" HARDBOARD

PLYWOOD LAYOUT
A: Cabinet sides, 22" x 30"
B: Cabinet tops, 22" x 24"
C: Drawer fronts (or door), 23⅞" x 24"
D: Toe kicks, 5" x 24"
E: Drawer backs & sides, see chart above
F: Drawer bottoms (when dadoed), 17" x 22¼"
G: Cabinet backs, 24" x 30"
H: Shelves, 17½" x 24"

assemble them. Round all four corners of the tops, side panels, and front panels. Notice drawer fronts are only rounded at their topmost and bottommost corners.

To round them, measure in 1½" from adjacent sides and, using a compass set at 1½", mark the quarter circle. Cut along the line, using any curve-cutting saw (page 19), and sand to smooth roundness.

Also cut the door and the center drawers' handpulls. (You only need to cut them for the center drawer because both the top and bottom drawer are pulled out by their lower edges.) Lay out the handpulls as shown in the sketch.

5 Add bottom spacers. A spacer cut from ¾" plywood is installed at the bottom of each unit to insure a uniform 24" spacing from top to bottom between the cabinet's side panels. Each spacer is 5" by 24" and is screwed to two small blocks of ¾" plywood (1½" by 5") that are permanently glued and nailed with 3d finish nails to the cabinet's sides. By using screws to fasten the spacer, the cabinet is demountable. Before installing the blocks, line them up beneath the spacer the way they will fit together in the unit and pre-drill the four screw holes, using a ⅛" bit.

6 Fasten the back. What the back is screwed to depends upon whether the cabinet has drawers or shelves inside. Drill holes and screw it to the back ends of drawer runners, shelves, shelf supports, or a small piece of molding inside. Inset the back 1½" so it can't be seen from the side.

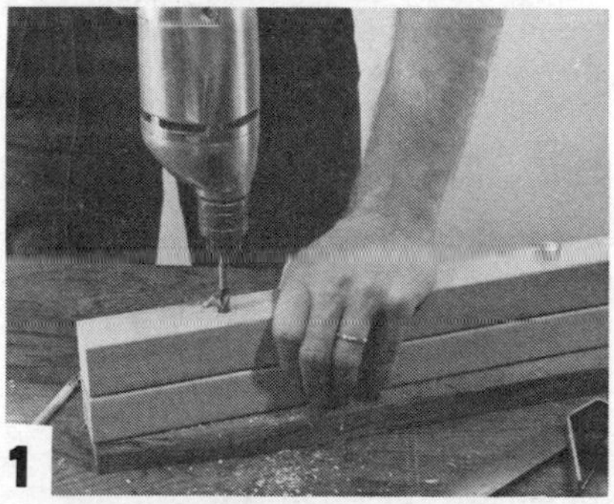
1

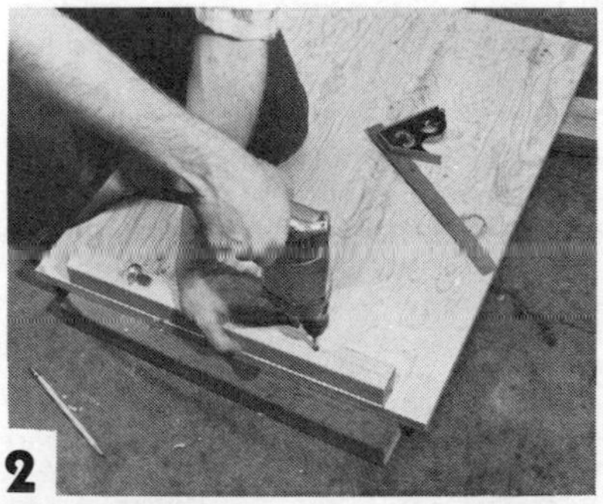
2

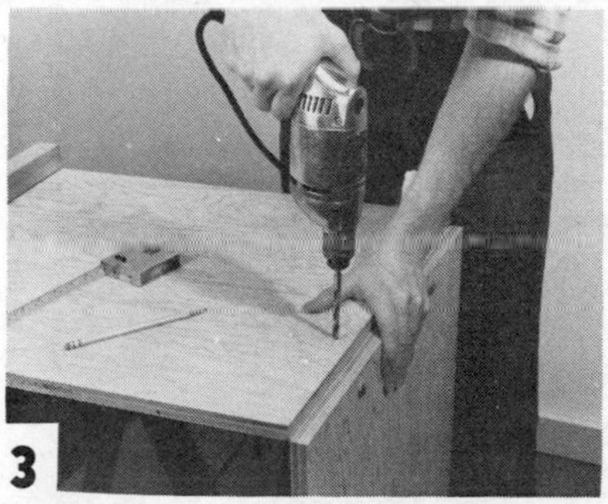
3

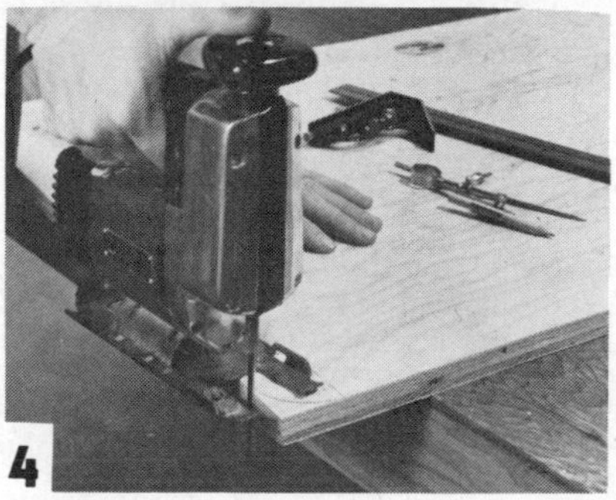
4

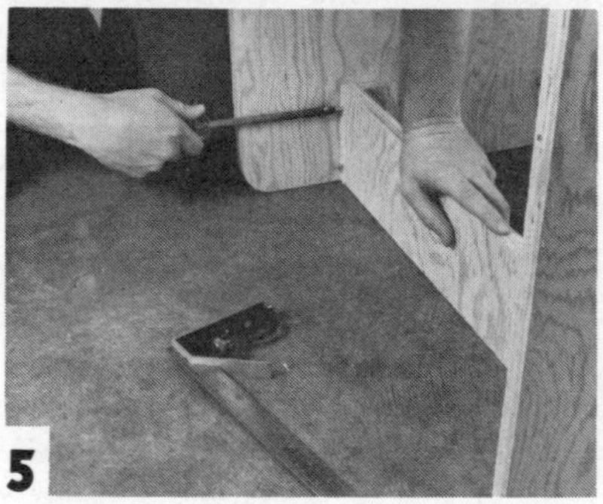
5

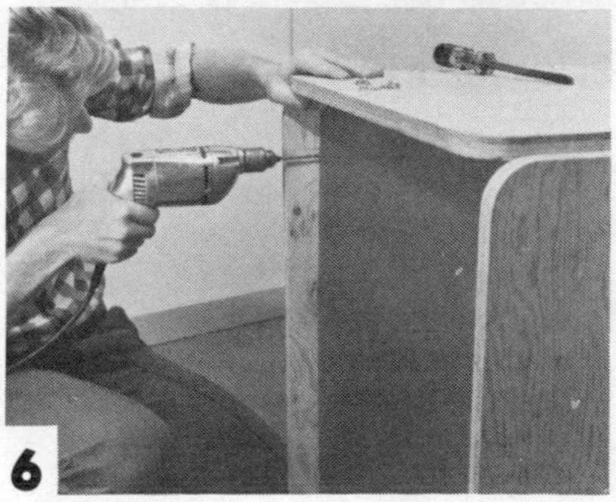
6

Built-in cabinet saves space

A speakeasy in miniature, this cabinet is the family saloon when open, part of the wall when buttoned up. Or for those who don't partake of spirits, the cabinet can serve as a small telephone desk, as kitchen storage with a drop-down counter, or as a child's flop-down desk. A built-in cabinet squeezes in storage where space is a problem; the wall absorbs most of the space the cabinet needs. At the same time, the wall provides basic framing for the cabinet, saving material costs.

To build-in a cabinet, you must plan its placement, remove part of the wall covering, reframe the opening to fit the cabinet, assemble and install the cabinet, add molding around its perimeter, and then give it a finish. Before starting work, read over the following construction details carefully.

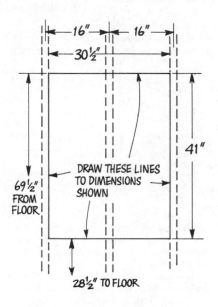

TOOLS YOU'LL NEED

To build-in a cabinet, you'll need a pencil, measuring tool, square, handsaw (a circular saw with masonry blade is very helpful), and a hammer. For this cabinet, other helpful tools include a nailset, screwdriver, hacksaw (for cutting the hinge), and finishing tools.

MATERIALS

The cabinet shown requires the following materials: 10' of construction-grade 2 by 4 (cut-out studs can be reused); 31' of clear 1 by 6; ½ sheet of A-A plywood; a 3' continuous hinge with ¾" screws; two magnetic cabinet catches with ¾" screws; a door pull; two 14" table stay supports with ¾" screws; four 1' shelf standards with tabs and 1" screws; 6d finishing nails; 16d box nails; patching compound; glue; and a finish.

HERE'S HOW

Choose a wall for the cabinet where electrical or plumbing fixtures won't intrude. Be sure to check the other side of the wall, too — and while you're there, consider the patchup and painting required if nails pull through from the side you're working on (reframing may cause this to happen). Also consider the cabinet's swing-down door — will anything obstruct it?

1 Find the approximate placement of wall studs inside the wall (see page 50). If the studs are spaced 16" apart center-to-center, like those in most walls, you'll only need to cut and remove part of one stud to leave the proper 30½" opening between studs. If studs are not on 16" centers (near another wall, door, or window), change the cabinet's dimensions to fit between studs. One word of caution: unless you can enlist the aid of a carpenter, your cabinet should not require the removal of more than two studs or be wider than four feet.

2 Draw two vertical lines on the wall where the cabinet's outside perimeters should be. These lines may be adjusted after the initial layout. Duplicate

the measurements and lines shown in the sketch. After drawing the first horizontal line, check it for level. If it isn't level, either the floor isn't level or you've measured incorrectly.

If neither floor nor ceiling is level, you may want to adjust all of the horizontal lines *very slightly* so the cabinet won't appear tilted. Don't over-adjust or objects will roll off of the finished cabinet's shelves and work surface.

3 Opening up the wall is a messy job — lay a tarpaulin or sheet of polyethylene on the floor to catch debris. The method you should use to locate precisely the wall studs that will stand at the cabinet's two sides will depend upon the wall-covering material.

For gypsum wallboard ("drywall"), knock a hole to the inside but near one of the two outer studs and continue the hole until you reach the stud's inner face. Measure from there 30½" to find the other stud's placement (presuming that the studs are spaced evenly on 16" centers). Make sure the second stud is beneath your measure by knocking a hole to the inside of that measurement and enlarging it toward the stud.

For plaster, the procedure is basically the same, but knock a small hole and use a screwdriver to probe for the side studs between the wood or wire lath.

Make sure the two vertical lines drawn on the wall are flush with the inner face of each side stud.

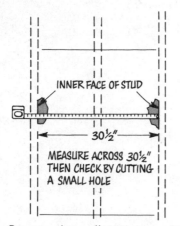

INNER FACE OF STUD

30½"

MEASURE ACROSS 30½" THEN CHECK BY CUTTING A SMALL HOLE

Remove the wall covering, cutting along the top, bottom, and two side lines. For plaster on wire lath, a circular saw with masonry blade is best — it cuts through both plaster and wire, allowing you to pull both out at once (be sure to wear eye protection when cutting). The same tool works well for cutting gypsum wallboard. A crosscut or keyhole saw will also cut wallboard, but because the material has a ground-rock core, it will dull the saw's blade (use an old blade). For a very clean cut in wallboard, first scribe the line with a knife. For plaster on wood lath, cut the lath with a regular saw after cutting the plaster with a masonry-cutting blade. Take care not to run the wood-cutting blade over any plaster.

4 Remove any fireblocking connected to the exposed center stud. Squarely cut off the center stud at the top and bottom perimeter marks (28½" and 69½" above the floor), using a handsaw (a short one is easiest to use). Make the bottom cut first, being sure to make the cuts complete.

Knock the cut stud back and forth in a slapping motion. This movement may ease the wood from nails holding the wall material to the stud's backside. If it doesn't, you'll pull the nails through

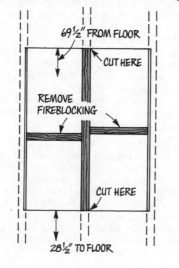

69½" FROM FLOOR

CUT HERE

REMOVE FIREBLOCKING

CUT HERE

28½" TO FLOOR

the backside wall material (use spackling compound to fill the resulting holes). Don't pry against the backside wall when removing the stud — you could push through it.

If the cabinet's placement doesn't fall between 16-inch-spaced studs, you may need to cut and remove a second stud at this time.

Cut two 2 by 4s that, when nailed together, will serve as a header between the two outside studs. Nail it together with 10d nails. Toenail the header in

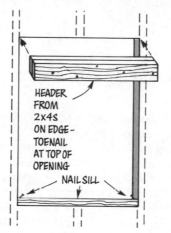

HEADER FROM 2x4s ON EDGE— TOENAIL AT TOP OF OPENING

NAIL SILL

place at the top of the opening, using 16d nails, as shown. Cut another 2 by 4 the same length and nail it in place (flat) at the bottom of the opening.

5 Before making the cabinet, check the measurement of the opening. Consider any inaccuracies or differences when cutting the cabinet's pieces and measure everything two or three times before cutting. (Although you can narrow the wall's opening with small pieces of wood, enlarging the opening is very difficult.)

Cut two 35¾-inch-long 1 by 6s for the frame's sides and two 30¼-inch-long 1 by 6s for the top and bottom. Miter cut the corners at 45° for a particularly goodlooking joint (otherwise, butt-join the corners). Sand all wooden pieces before assembling.

Nail the 1 by 6s together with 6d finishing nails, holding the edges flush and the corners "square." Cut the ⅜" plywood back to 35¾" by 30¼", the grain running the long dimension. Be sure it is "square." Nail the back to the frame, good-side forward, using 6d finish nails. The back should pull the cabinet into true square as you nail. Check this box frame's fit in the opening.

The size to cut the ¾" plywood door will depend upon the way you treat the raw plywood edges (see page 10). If you use some type of molding, adjust the finished dimensions of the door to include the additional thickness of the molding. If you use veneer tape or nothing, no adjustment is necessary.

The door's finished dimensions should be 30¼" by 27½".

Fasten the continuous hinge to the frame's bottom as shown below (you may have to cut it with a hacksaw). Align the door's edges with the frame's sides, butt the door firmly against the hinge pin, and put a screw in at each end. Close the door to make sure the door's edges are flush with the frame; if they're not flush, adjust the corner screws until they are. Then add the rest of the screws.

Cut a 28¾" shelf from the 1 by 6 and nail it so that its top is flush with the top edge of the door when the door is shut. Fasten magnetic catches on the underside of this shelf.

Screw a pair of 12" shelf brackets to each side of the frame, butted against the top shelf's underside. Cut one or two removable shelves (about 27¾").

6 Place the cabinet in the opening and nail it in place with four or five 6d finishing nails, setting the heads. Secure the stay hinges to the frame, making sure they will clear the cabinet's bottom when the door is closed (about 1½" from front edge). Extend one hinge fully and, holding the door level, hold the other end on the door and try the door's action. When it works properly, screw it onto the door. Repeat with the other hinge.

Add a pull to the door and cut and nail the trim in place around the cabinet. Use a 1 by 6 over and under, a 1 by 2 on each side. Finish as desired.

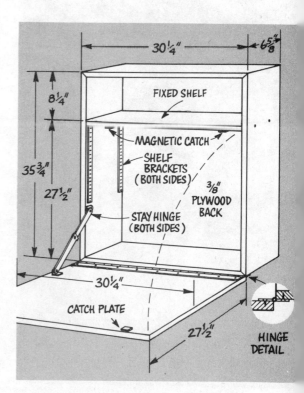

30¼"

6⅝"

8¼"

FIXED SHELF

MAGNETIC CATCH

SHELF BRACKETS (BOTH SIDES)

35¾"

27½"

⅜" PLYWOOD BACK

STAY HINGE (BOTH SIDES)

30¼"

CATCH PLATE

27½"

HINGE DETAIL

Serving cart rolls to guests

Laden with drinks, glasses, an ice bucket, chips and dips, or hors d'oeuvres, this snappy serving cart usually shines as the life of the party.

Made primarily from one sheet of plywood and a chopping-block top, the roll-around serving cart is strong and relatively easy to make. Cutting out the pieces is probably the most difficult part, but even this is easy if you have a power saw. Otherwise, you can have the lumberyard make the major cuts. Assembling it with glue and nails is simple. (Look for a color photograph of this unit on the back cover.) Design: Donald Wm. Mac-Donald, AIA.

TOOLS YOU'LL NEED

Unless most pieces are cut at the lumberyard, a good saw is very necessary. A saber saw will cut the curves, cutouts, and, when used with a guide, the straight lines. Also have a pencil, measuring tool, square, compass, hammer, nailset (or large nail), screwdriver, sandpaper and finishing tools, metal-cutting saw (to cut the continuous hinges to length), and chisel (for mortising the turnbuckles' hooks into the top's underside). For a decorative effect, you can round exposed plywood edges, using a router and ⅜" edge-rounding bit.

MATERIALS

The following materials are needed for the cart: one sheet of ¾" A-A plywood (birch veneered plywood was used), two feet of 1 by 10 for the adjustable shelf, two feet of 1 by 12 for the glass-storage bottom, a 1' by 5' hardwood chopping block top (cut into three sections, as shown), six L-brackets, four casters, four shelf brackets with clips, six 2" by ¾" fixed-pin butt hinges, 2' of continuous (piano) hinge with 1" or ¾" butts, two hooks, two eyes, two turnbuckles, two wooden knobs, a roll of leather thonging or heavy colored cord, a box of 6d finishing nails, wood putty, and paint.

HERE'S HOW

Cut the plywood according to the diagram. If possible, have the lumberyard attendants make the two major cuts (the rip down the center and the main crosscut). Some lumberyards carry chopping blocks in standard sizes; the one shown was purchased from a cabinetmaker. It's wise to have the lumberyard or cabinetmaker cut it precisely into its three sections after building the cart.

1 Begin with the side panels (A). Cut the handle holes and top-support brackets according to the sketch. A saber saw works best, but a keyhole saw will also do the job (finish the long, straight cuts with a handsaw). Begin the handle-hole cuts from small holes drilled in the waste wood; start the support bracket cuts from the ½" finger holes specified.

2 Duplicate the marks in the sketch onto the inside surface of one of the side panels. Clamp that panel flushly to its mate and drill ⅛" holes every 4" between the lines, penetrating both panels (put a scrap beneath the lower panel so you don't break away the wood or drill into your work surface). Be sure to drill the holes straight. The holes drilled into the lower panel eliminate the need for marking that panel and make nailing easier. After drilling all the holes, unclamp the pieces and set the unmarked panel aside.

If you plan to round exposed plywood edges using a router, do it before assembling the unit.

3 Glue and nail the bottom panel (C) to the marked side panel. For fastening all permanent shelves and dividers in the cabinet, use glue and 2" (6d) finishing nails, setting the nail heads below the surface. Glue and nail the lower back panel (I) to the bottom panel and side panel. Putting a block beneath it as shown will raise the level slightly for easier nailing.

4 Glue and nail the glass-storage shelf (J) to the side panel and lower back panel; then glue and nail the lower divider (D) to the side panel and the glass-storage shelf.

5 Glue and nail the midshelf (B) to the side panel and lower divider. Glue and toenail the outer edge of the upper divider (H) to the midshelf; then nail the divider to the side panel. Add the glass and bottle-holding lips (E and F). Set all nails.

Lay the unit on its side, spread glue along all of the exposed edges of shelves and dividers, lay the other side panel into position, and nail it. Set all of the nail heads.

6 Attach the two support flaps, using butt hinges as shown in the sketch. Cut continuous hinges to the width of the cutting board (12") and screw them in place, as shown.

Attach the top temporarily, using L-brackets as shown (you may want to remove the top when painting the unit). Add the turnbuckle flap supports, also shown. Screw the furniture casters to the bottom of the unit, insetting them about 1" from all edges; fasten the shelf brackets inside the unit for the shelf (K); and hinge the doors (G) on the front, using butt hinges (page 43). You can either add knobs for door pulls or drill finger holes (2" diameter).

Sand and paint the unit, being careful not to paint the butcher block top. Then spiral the handles with leather thonging or heavy cord (tack or glue it in place or knot it in drilled holes at each end).

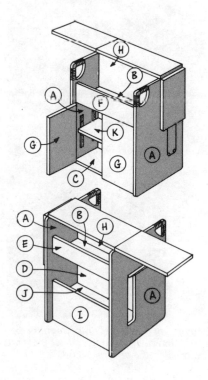

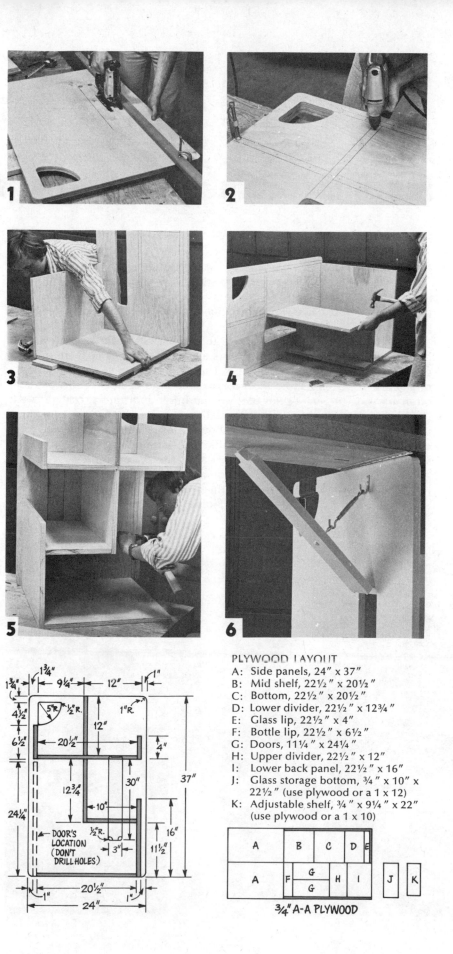

PLYWOOD LAYOUT

A: Side panels, 24" x 37"
B: Mid shelf, 22½" x 20½"
C: Bottom, 22½" x 20½"
D: Lower divider, 22½" x 12¾"
E: Glass lip, 22½" x 4"
F: Bottle lip, 22½" x 6½"
G: Doors, 11¼" x 24¼"
H: Upper divider, 22½" x 12"
I: Lower back panel, 22½" x 16"
J: Glass storage bottom, ¾" x 10" x 22½" (use plywood or a 1 x 12)
K: Adjustable shelf, ¾" x 9¼" x 22" (use plywood or a 1 x 10)

¾" A-A PLYWOOD

Modular cabinets for kitchens

New homes and remodels often have kitchen cabinets just like these. A version of the basic face-frame cabinet shown on page 40, they are actually a system of several fairly small units that fit together. Some are cupboards for shelves, others hold drawers, and still others are made to accept built-in appliances. Although the cabinets shown have smooth, undecorated faces, a bit of decorative wood trim glued to the doors can customize them to your tastes.

Their modular construction makes them ideal for do-it-yourselfers. You can make them in a shop or outdoors and then easily carry them one-by-one into the kitchen for installation. Their adjustability covers a multitude of sins — they don't show the gaps between the cabinets and walls that often appear. The bug-a-boos of flush and offset doors are also eliminated: these doors are easy to make and install, and they will never stick or show uneven cracks. A bonus is that the beveled-edge door and drawer fronts don't need pulls or handles. And if, after use, you find that one of the doors should have been hinged on the other side, simply reverse it.

Although you can order these modular cabinets from some lumberyards and install them yourself, building them can be considerably less expensive. Following is a discussion of building methods.

TOOLS AND MATERIALS

The complexity of construction and the number of necessary tools will depend upon the particular cabinets you build. Those shown here are merely meant to serve as an example. You'll need a fairly complete tool box: such tools as a pencil, square, measuring tape, hammer, nailset, screwdriver, drill, and a good saw. The saw should be a portable power saw with a bevel adjustment, a table saw, or a radial-arm saw.

The materials are discussed throughout the following instructions. Plan your cabinets on paper so you can calculate the amount and types of materials you'll need.

Stove unit easily fits into opening between modular cabinets. All cabinets are built using the same methods.

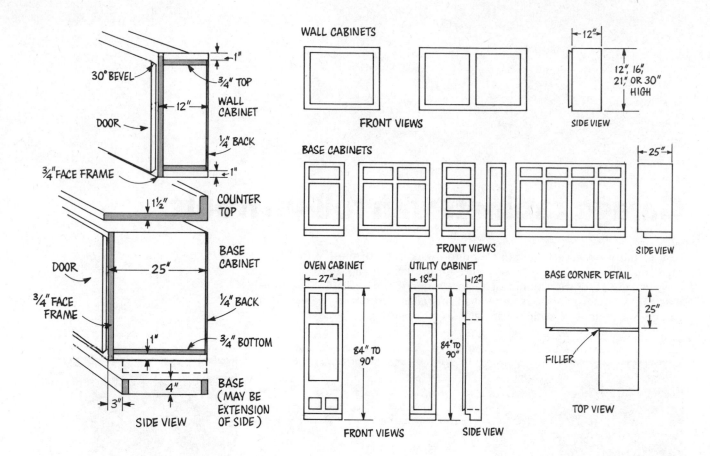

HERE'S HOW

Make the cabinets of ⅝" or ¾" plywood or particle board (you may wish to use the type veneered with a thin outer layer of plastic laminate, shown in the top photograph on page 12). If you make the cabinets from a material that will be painted, you won't need to cover the plywood edges later in their construction. (See information on treating exposed plywood edges of cabinets taking natural or semi-transparent finishes on page 10.) Use 6d finishing nails and white glue for assembling most of the pieces.

The separate bases beneath all of the lower cabinets are simply open frames made from ¾" plywood or 2 by 4s. Make them as shown. Allow for a toe space in front of each base cabinet by insetting the frame 3". Position the base and nail it to floor joists; then slip the completed base cabinets over the base and nail them to it. If the floor is uneven, level the bases by driving shingles under them. Hide any resulting spaces along the floor with a rubber baseboard.

Base cabinets are made as illustrated (also see page 40). Match dimensions to your sink, disposal, dishwasher, range, and refrigerator. Allow about 1½" extra for the refrigerator's width so it can be rolled in place easily and so its door will have room to swing. By making the shelves inside cabinets adjustable, you can vary their heights or add more at any time (see page 45 for information on mounting shelves in cabinets). Consider the height of the person who will use the counters. If he or she is tall, add an extra inch to the base cabinets' height. Notice that the ¼" cabinet backs are cut 1" shorter than the sides — the back sits flush on the base; the sides overlap it 1". For pipes or wiring, cut any holes in the backs of cabinets extra large so the cabinets will slip into place easily.

Drawers and doors for the cabinets can be made like those discussed on pages 46-48 and pages 42-44. For these cabinets, metal center guides for drawers work well. To cut the beveled edges of the drawer and door fronts, you'll need a table saw, radial-arm saw, or portable power saw with bevel adjustment. If you don't have one of these, cut the edges square and paint or treat the plywood edges. Then add door pulls (page 44). Self-closing ⅜" offset cabinet hinges used on the doors eliminate the need for catches.

Countertops are separate from the cabinets. They run full length, capping a bank of cabinets in one stretch. Although you can make them yourself from plastic laminated ¾" plywood or particle board, built up to a 1½" thickness with 1 by 3s below, cutting the laminated top smoothly usually requires a tungsten-carbide blade. So consider having a cabinet shop make them and cut out the sink hole. Screw and glue the top to the completed cabinets from below.

Wall cabinets are made like the base cabinets, but both their tops and bottoms are recessed 1" into the sides, as shown in the drawing. It's wise to make the inner shelves adjustable. Build the cabinets about 31" high and, when wall-mounting them, leave a 17" or 18" working space below. The cabinet that fits over a range hood should be shorter. Nail the wall and base cabinets securely to wall studs, particularly along the top (see page 50).

Garage cabinets with roll-up fronts

Easy to build because they don't require doors, each of these 8-foot-long plywood cabinets has a colorful canvas front that rolls up and out of the way, making all of the cabinet's contents exposed and available. The cabinets can store an enormous amount of miscellany up out of the way in a garage (most double garages can take six of them).

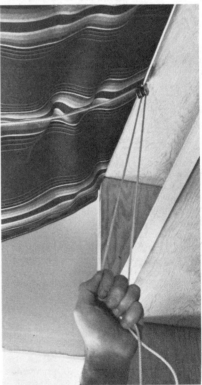

Canvas curtains *roll up backwards; pulleys and most cords are hidden inside the cabinet under the 1 by 2 trim.*

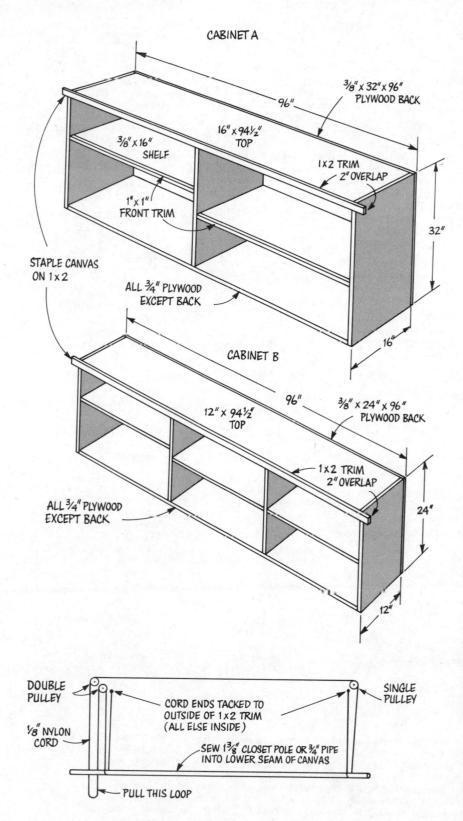

CABINET A

96"

³⁄₈" x 32" x 96"
PLYWOOD BACK

16" x 94½"
TOP

³⁄₈" x 16"
SHELF

1 x 2 TRIM
2" OVERLAP

1" x 1"
FRONT TRIM

32"

STAPLE CANVAS
ON 1 x 2

ALL ¾" PLYWOOD
EXCEPT BACK

16"

CABINET B

96"

12" x 94½"
TOP

³⁄₈" x 24" x 96"
PLYWOOD BACK

1 x 2 TRIM
2" OVERLAP

24"

ALL ¾" PLYWOOD
EXCEPT BACK

12"

DOUBLE
PULLEY

SINGLE
PULLEY

CORD ENDS TACKED TO
OUTSIDE OF 1 x 2 TRIM
(ALL ELSE INSIDE)

⅛" NYLON
CORD

SEW 1³⁄₈" CLOSET POLE OR ¾" PIPE
INTO LOWER SEAM OF CANVAS

PULL THIS LOOP

TOOLS AND MATERIALS

Typical tools needed for making these cabinets include a pencil, measuring tool, square, saw, hammer, and screwdriver. Helpful tools to have on hand are a staple gun and a ladder.

The necessary materials will depend upon the size and number of cabinets you make. For either type of cabinet, you'll need one 100" length of 1" by 2" wood trim, one 100" length of 1³⁄₈" closet pole or ¾" pipe, 100 inches of 1-yard-wide canvas, a ball of ⅛" nylon cord, one single and one double pulley, glue, 6d nails, and 10d common nails or 3" screws.

The type "A" cabinet also requires one 4' by 8' sheet of ¾" plywood, one 4' by 8' sheet of ³⁄₈" plywood, and 8' of 1" by 1" molding (for trim).

The type "B" cabinet requires one 4' by 8' sheet of ¾" plywood and one 2' by 8' (half sheet) of ³⁄₈" plywood.

HERE'S HOW

Dimension the cabinets in either of the two ways shown in the large illustrations. This way, you'll have practically no wastage of plywood. The "A" cabinet fits high-ceiling garages; the smaller "B" version will still leave a 6' headroom in an 8-foot-high garage. Make some of the shelves adjustable (see page 45) to fit odd-sized items.

In hanging the cabinets, use a brace, as shown in the photograph, and nail

or screw them securely to wall studs (see page 50). Seam a loop along the bottom edge of the canvas for the closet pole or pipe to slide through; then staple the top edge of the canvas to the underside of the 1 by 2 trim. Also attach the pulleys for the pull cords to the underside of the trim.

Index

PHOTOGRAPHERS

Ernest Braun: 21 upper center, bottom; 77 top right. **Carla Cannon:** 79 center. **Glenn Christiansen:** 15; 57 top left; 64; 65 top left. **Roger Flanagan:** 72; 73. **Ells Marugg:** 8; 10; 11; 12; 18 bottom; 20 bottom right; 21 top, lower center; 22 top; 23 top center, bottom center, bottom right; 25; 30 bottom left and center; 31; 33; 34; 38; 39; 40; 56; 57 right; 62; 63; 68; 69; 71 center, bottom; 74; 75; 82 top; 83 top left, center left, center; 86; 87; 90; 91; 92; 94; 95; back cover. **Jack McDowell:** 22 bottom. **Norman A. Plate:** 18 top; 19 top right, left, center; 20 top, bottom left; 49 right; 57 bottom left; 66 bottom; 67; 70; 71 top; 76 right; 77 bottom left; 84; 85. **Richard Red:** 88. **Martha Rosman:** 49 left. **Mike Tilden:** 65 top, bottom right. **Donald W. Vandervort:** 24; 29; 76 left. **Darrow M. Watt:** 18 center; 23 top right, top left, bottom left; 30 right column; 44; 49 center; 55; 66 top; 77 top left, bottom right; 78; 79 top; 80; 81. **Peter Whiteley:** 82 bottom. **Craig Zwicky:** 83 bottom.